GREAT PLANTING

GREAT PLANTING

LUCY GENT

WARD LOCK

To the ever-appreciative National Gardens Scheme visitor

A WARD LOCK BOOK

First published in the UK 1995
by Ward Lock
Wellington House
125 Strand
LONDON
WC2R 0BB

A Cassell Imprint
Volume copyright © Ward Lock 1995
Text © Lucy Gent 1995

Distributed in the United States
by Sterling Publishing Co., Inc.
387 Park Avenue South, New York, NY 10016–8810

Distributed in Australia
by Capricorn Link (Australia) Pty Ltd
2/13 Carrington Road, Castle Hill NSW 2154

A British Library Cataloguing in Publication Data block for this book may be obtained from the British Library

ISBN 0 7063 7351 0

Commissioning Editor: Stuart Cooper
Managing Editor: Jane Birch
Project Editor: Lydia Darbyshire
Design: Town Group Consultancy
Picture Researcher: Emily Hedges

Printed and bound in Spain

HALF-TITLE PAGE: Verbascums and sisyrinchium against a foil of dark berberis at Denmans, Sussex.
TITLE PAGE: Iris, marguerites and orange erysimum in Monet's garden. Clarity of plant form underlines the use of colours that intensify each other.

CONTENTS

Introduction

A great garden is a synthesis of design and planting. But although long-established principles may be applied in garden design, excellence in planting is harder to define and still more difficult to achieve. Successful planting requires both horticultural skill and an artistic eye to select plants that will create an effective composition, and today this is more difficult than ever before. There are so many plants to choose from, and so many gardening philosophies, too.

Part I of *Great Planting* shows how this situation has come about. From the sixteenth century onwards plant hunters and hybridizers made more and more plants available to the gardener. As long as formality in the garden was the aim, a rule of thumb existed for the arrangement of both native and exotic plants. But once landscape design began to favour naturalism in the eighteenth century, this guide lost its force, while nature turned out to provide no substitute rules.

Only at the end of the nineteenth century did design principles in planting begin to re-emerge, and these, first voiced by Gertrude Jekyll, have been confidently developed during the twentieth century. At the same time, the phenomenal successes of horticulture have continued to woo the gardener, while the last few decades have also seen an increasing trend towards natural-looking planting. As a result, today's gardener is faced with a wonderful, but somewhat confusing, wealth of choice.

Great Planting shows a way through this embarrassment of riches, by means of the dual tools of intention and selection. Part II looks at the how these were enunciated for the twentieth century by Gertrude Jekyll in Britain and by Beatrix Farrand in the United States. It then examines a range of late twentieth-century versions of excellence in planting. These include examples of informal styles, such as the cottage garden, ecological planting, and gardens made from plants taken from the wild. Interspersed are gardens where the guiding principle is that of artistry, for the idea that individual artists or artistic movements can help us see and choose is a major theme of the book. Colour, that perennial lure and challenge, is carefully analysed, along with more recent trends, such as the use of large-leaves in planting.

Regarding each garden from a particular stylistic angle can help us to understand why the planting is as it is and why it works so well. Gardens are, however, the result of many factors, and no planting is going to fit into one category only. Beth Chatto's gravel garden is an example of planting in a dry landscape, but it is also an illustration of ecological awareness.

Part III sets out the principles of planting, looking at elements such as structure, texture and colour that can, to some extent, help us to define today's ideas of excellence in planting.

Although it is broad in scope, this book is one person's view. Someone else would make different choices and lay the emphasis differently. Formality, for example, is not treated separately, although it is illustrated in a variety of contexts.

Through descriptions, photographs and plans, *Great Planting* shows how the criteria of clear intentions, selection guided by a thoughtful eye and sensitivity to landscape – criteria that are available to all of us – can lead to planting with claims to the title of 'great'. It also looks forward to the next century by highlighting the inspiration to be found in many new planting experiments as well as in the examples of the past.

OPPOSITE: Overflowing melianthus foliage is the star in this corner of Beth Chatto's gravel garden, surrounded by the rich detailing of sedums and the contrasting spikes of kniphofias.

PART I
THE STORY OF GREAT PLANTING

ABOVE: Great swathes of grasses and
sedums match the scale of the American
landscape in this garden designed by
Oehme and van Sweden.

OPPOSITE: Plenty of space is provided in this
garden for the simple magnificence of the
dark-leaved form of *Sambucus nigra*.

Great Planting: Standards or Taste?

What one person regards as great planting, another might think is perfectly frightful. The Victorians, for example, doted on bedding schemes and on monkey puzzle trees, which today are thought of as uninspiring and over regimented. A twelfth-century monk would probably regard with horror the Australasian cordylines and phormiums that nowadays command admiration, just as medieval tastes formed on Gregorian chant would find Beethoven symphonies cacophonous. For the traditional Japanese gardener,

A classic herbaceous border at Jenkyn Place, where a sombre yew hedge and crisp paths are a foil to rich colours. Clouds of *Crambe cordifolia* flowers invite the eye to rest.

used to the austere simplicities of rock and stone, and moss and water, much European planting is garish. Great planting is ultimately a matter of taste.

Today's ideas of great planting might include the classic herbaceous borders of Jenkyn Place at Bentley in Hampshire; a private garden in London where a vast honey-scented *Euphorbia mellifera* in a courtyard is beautifully in tune with the brick and paving; one of Christopher Lloyd's paradisal meadows at Great Dixter in Sussex; the ancient yew hedges of Powis Castle in Wales; or a border skilfully cultivated by the Dutch painter Ton ter Linden in warm oranges and yellows. Many of us would admire the traditional abundance of the cottage garden, while others revere

These monumental yew hedges at Powis Castle provide simplicity and, because of their age, rich associations.

those avenues of limes leading to some hidden country house. A simple reason for considering all these styles 'great' is because they create harmony in the way that the planting is attuned to the setting.

It is doubtful if Edinburgh's famous brightly coloured floral clock, which gives pleasure to many people, would be considered great today. If that is so, what are the standards set by designers and gardeners? Do such planting schemes lack the sort of harmony that is prized today? Perhaps snobbery has something to answer for.

What we admire in planting now is shaped by many factors. One is availability, which follows from the history of plant introductions from other continents around the world, and then the excitements of plant breeding and hybridizing. The story here is one of an accelerating wealth of choice. A second influence is the recurrent inspiration of nature, and the way that tastes have continually swung between formal planting and natural profusion. A third element is the influence of individuals in the garden world, which is as important in garden design as it is in all other aspects of changing fashion. Circles of friendship, publications, horticultural events and, in the later twentieth century, the media, are the channels by which their effect is felt. Again the tale is one of an ever-increasing ease of access to new ideas. All such factors – plant availability, oscillations in taste and the influence of talented individuals – are closely intertwined.

Plant Availability and the Problem of Selection

Garden planting in medieval Britain was simple because it consisted of a restricted range of local species together with a few common European species. The Romans started it. They introduced box, bay and juniper to Britain when they began to settle in the first century. Rosemary did not cross the English Channel with them, but it was growing in Britain by 1340. The herbs for cooking and for medicine that figured in every garden were largely native, but this is not to say that they were planted without regard for patterning and a pleasing lay-out. Orchards, for example, were established as a form of ornamental planting by the Middle Ages in England, and training and clipping were commonplace.

A medieval enclosed garden with daisies underfoot and other simple plants in formal beds. Trees play an important part in the planting, while elaboration is provided by the fountain and the trellis.

The English Channel, formed at the end of the Ice Age, prevented many species from reaching Britain, but in Europe the range of plant options was greater. In addition, the climate was warmer further south, permitting greater diversity. More plants had been introduced from the East by the Middle Ages. Irises, carnations and the idea of the flowery meadow had also arrived in southern France. There, too, an extensive range of fruit and vegetables was grown, including pomegranates, grapes and figs, which can be glimpsed in the pleasure gardens that are shown in illuminated manuscripts.

The entertaining history of the tulip illustrates an early phase in plant collecting and plant manias. It was introduced into Europe from Turkey about 1570, and the name *Tulipa clusiana* is a reminder of the role played by Charles de L'Ecluse (1526–1609) in introducing day-lilies, crown imperials, narcissi, hyacinths and many other then exotic plants into Europe. Tulipomania swept the Netherlands in the 1630s, when collectors avidly pursued the results of spontaneously occurring viruses, eventually giving the humble tulip the status of currency.

If plant enthusiasts went first in search of new specimens to the Middle East, they soon travelled to other parts of the world: North America, South Africa and, by the nineteenth century, China and the Himalayas became favoured terrains. In the late eighteenth century, with the voyages of men like Joseph Banks, Australia was added to the list. Rhododendrons and camellias became fashionable in the early nineteenth century. The introduction of new species was facilitated by the invention of the Wardian case in the 1830s. Nathaniel Ward (1791–1868) built a device that enabled transported plants to live indefinitely, since the water they transpired was condensed and re-used.

A roll-call of only a few names serves as a reminder of what we owe to the plant collectors: *Drimys winteri* (Captain Winter, 1575), the fuchsia (Leonhart Fuchs, 1501–66), the lobelia (Matthias de l'Obel,

The great plant illustrator Georg Dionysius Ehret (1708–70) does full justice to the tulip's beauty of form, with a precision that is almost passionate.

1538–1616), tradescantia (John Tradescant, 1608–62), *Rosa banksia* (Captain Banks in the 1760s), *Geranium wallichianum* (Nathaniel Wallich in the 1820s), *Asarum hartwegii* (Theodor Hartweg, 1830s), *Paeonia*

The West owes *Paeonia mlokosewitschii,* with its enchanting ephemeral flowers and clear, light green foliage, to the Russian collector, Mlokosewitsch.

veitchii (James Veitch, 1815–69), *Hosta fortunei* (Robert Fortune, 1813–69, who also introduced the yellow winter jasmine), *Viburnum farreri* (Reginald Farrer, 1913–20), *Sorbus vilmorinii* (Pierre Philippe André de Vilmorin, 1776–1862, of the famous French family of nurserymen) and *Sorbus intermedia* 'Joseph Rock' (which celebrates the American plant hunter of that name, 1884–1962). And it continues today, with *Euphorbia schillingii,* which was named after Tony Schilling. This selection of names signals the role of collectors, patrons and gardeners in introducing

increasing numbers of exotic subjects into western Europe. Such names, of course, represent only a tiny proportion of the plants collected.

With the development of greenhouse technology in the nineteenth century, the cultivation and overwintering of pelargoniums and other tender and tropical species became possible, and the large-scale propagation of such colourful plants as calceolarias, salvias, lobelias, echeverias and begonias supplied the various bedding-out crazes that flourished between 1820 and 1890.

Alongside ever-increasing introductions into western Europe of new plants, skills in plant propagation and hybridization were developing. While the technique of grafting was established early on, the first plant hybrid was recorded in 1717. Thereafter hybridization was a major growth area. In the 1840s the transformation of Kew Gardens in London into a centre of science and horticulture gave the official stamp of approval to the use of technology in the service of gardens.

The relevance of all this to 'great planting' is that horticultural success led to the collapse of principles of choice. Nineteenth-century English gardeners could be compared to the Middle Eastern carpet makers who, once introduced to gaudy chemical dyes, found that their customary earth colours and plant dyes such as indigo and madder, lacked glamour. They enthusiastically took up the new magentas and scarlets and blues. Access to the cornucopia, in carpets as in plants, must have been a wonderful experience. It still is today, but the problem is that it disorientates any older harmonies in planting. New plant hybrids and arrivals continue to make choice more difficult, particularly when, with ultra-efficient propagation and advertising, they flood the market. Perhaps one of the reasons for the popularity of garden design today is that we feel it will help us to choose – either by the choice we practise as designers ourselves, or by the designer we choose to employ.

Cycles of Taste

Of all the factors that determine notions of 'greatness', the most intriguing is certainly the one that depends on fluctuations in taste. The history of planting style reveals a cycle of sophistication followed by the rediscovery of nature. Whether art or nature is in the ascendant depends perhaps on which you perceive yourself as having less of, since it will then be more desirable.

The cycle is already evident by the mid-seventeenth century when the poet Andrew Marvell grumbles against artifice and formality. He preferred the simple meadows:

> *Where willing nature does to all dispense*
> *A wild and fragrant innocence.*

Knot gardens using edgings of hyssop, thyme and lavender, had appeared in Europe – and England – by the beginning of the sixteenth century. By the seventeenth century they were a major fashion, with plantings of box and rosemary laid out to create elaborate geometrical shapes. The basic style of the upper class pleasure garden was formality, providing a framework for the display of exotic new introductions, accompanied by extravaganzas of garden architecture such as symbolic fountains.

How this style dominated can be seen in the bird's eye views of grand houses and their gardens by Jan Kyp

The planting in the Tudor Garden at Southampton, an accurate reconstruction of a sixteenth-century garden, provides formality and fantasy amid low-key colour. This harmony was to be shattered by exotic introductions in the nineteenth century.

(*c* 1652–1722). The natural landscape is excluded from these gardens, with their straight paths and straight lines of planting, not only physically by walls but also in spirit, for nature does not organize itself into such linearity. Such an exclusion had been implicit long before in the enclosed garden, the *hortus conclusus,* but the greater scale of the gardening around country houses, and the sustained and systematic formality of lay-out, suggests more of a break between garden landscape and the natural one outside the garden walls.

Through Kyp, too, we can gauge the popularity of the canal garden, imported from Holland, an example of which is to be found at Westbury Court in Gloucestershire, now carefully restored by the National Trust. Here a striking feature of the planting is the amount of yew hedging by the sides of the water.

In France, formality and the lay-out of the parterre persisted, but in England a reaction set in. William Kent (1685–1748) 'leaped the fence, and saw that all nature was a garden', in Horace Walpole's famous phrase. The naturalism practised by Lancelot 'Capability' Brown (1716–83) and Humphrey Repton (1752–1818) on the estates of the wealthy opened up carefully managed views of the surrounding countryside. Their handling of trees in relation to the contours of the landscape, often creating picturesque echoes of

ABOVE: At Westbury Court, Gloucestershire, formal yew hedging frames the canvas of the water's surface, reflecting an ever-changing sky.
BELOW: An eighteenth-century classical landscape at Stourhead, Wiltshire, is overlaid by layers of later, more colourful planting.

Unaffected profusion is the keynote of successful cottage-garden planting. Here the colours of aubrieta, myosotis and cheiranthus complement each other wonderfully.

landscape painting, still provides the twentieth century with standards of tree planting in the wider landscape, while Stourhead in Wiltshire is a haunting idyll, the trees, temples and lakes creating a classical vision.

Formality and artifice came to the fore once again in the planting style that typifies the nineteenth century, if only because of the scale on which exotics were being made available to gardeners. The arboretum rather than the copse is what the period is remembered for.

William Robinson's *The Wild Garden*, first published in 1870 (and last reprinted in 1983, such is its staying power) challenged the taste for what was exotic, helping also to make visible the informal style that had been there all the time, that is to say, the cottage garden. Whatever the realities of the cottager's poverty, the garden itself stood – and stands – for simplicity and naturalness. Here once again taste meets plant availability. For the contents of our gardens today are influenced by a range of herbaceous perennials preserved in cottage gardens in times when non-native plants pre-occupied

the fashion-conscious. You may remember Flora Thompson's description of the flowers in Old Sally's garden in *Lark Rise to Candleford*:

> …*such flowers, and so many of them, and nearly all of them sweet-scented! Wallflowers and tulips, lavender and sweet william, and pinks and old-world roses with enchanting names –* Seven Sisters, Maiden's Blush, *moss rose, monthly rose, cabbage rose, blood rose.*

Writing in 1962, the garden designer Russell Page describes how when he was a young man the plants he admired in the local Leicestershire market were not to be found in the gardens of family friends. 'They seemed to grow only in cottage gardens in hamlets lost among the fields and woods,' gardens that contained old-fashioned pinks and roses 'not to be found in any catalogue', and also 'seedlings of plants brought home perhaps by a sailor cousin'.

While the cottage garden endured, swings in taste between formal and informal continued. William Robinson was reacting to Victorian obsessions with horticulture and ornament from the viewpoint of a gardener. Sir Reginald Blomfield (1856–1942) reacted to the same imbalance but, as an architect, found the remedy in formal gardening that took architecture as its model. For him the essence of a garden lay in structure and shape, in its hard landscaping and in plants such as trimmed yew that assisted in realizing the formal garden as a work of art. He therefore strongly opposed the more naturalistic style advocated by Robinson.

This persistent cycle is complicated and overlaid by fashions that sweep into Europe and America as the result of technology and communications. Take, for example, the case of the alpine garden. Robinson's *Alpine Flowers for English Gardens,* published in 1870, wedded alpine flora to the rockeries that had existed since around 1800 but that by the late nineteenth century had become miniature mountains. Reginald Farrer's classic on alpines appeared in 1918, and rockeries for alpine subjects continued to be a desirable piece of garden furnishing for many decades. As late as the 1950s, Brigadier Lucas Phillips in his influential *Small Gardens* instructed his readers how to avoid the 'Here

lies poor Fido' look in making them. To grow alpines was to aspire to 'great planting'. Today, by contrast, their cultivation is seen as a special skill, which can, for example, be admired in the Edinburgh Botanic Garden, and in the hands of gifted amateurs.

In America a fashion for Japanese gardens has been much stronger than in Europe, and, as with alpines, might once have been taken as an area in which to display great planting. And of course there are superb 'Japanese' gardens in the United States, such as that in the Brooklyn Botanic Garden, where the quality of the planting is very high, even if it is not exactly the character of a garden that would be seen in Japan. But in its own way it is a symptom of the stylistic confusion that Russell Page noted in English gardens at the turn of the century. Amid many borrowed elements of design, he said, might be added 'picturesque themes such as wild-gardens, alpine gardens, heather gardens and bog gardens'.

Rocks and gravel are as important as mosses in Ryoan-ji Temple, Japan, where textures are crucial. The resultant simplicity allows room for numerous symbolic meanings.

Inspirational Individuals and the Diffusion of Ideas

Amid all the confusing options, there have been mentors, whose good sense and flair have guided friends, clients or readers, as the case may be. Thomas Loudon (1783–1843) and Jane Loudon (1807–58), for example, offered immense guidance through their books and periodicals on gardening in the nineteenth century, although now such figures are too remote to be seen as anything other than a part of history. With William Robinson, whose books are still read today, the influence can still be a quickening one, while his friend and disciple, Gertrude Jekyll (1843–1932), could well be regarded as the presiding genius in twentieth-century British planting.

The ease with which their names are associated masks a fundamental difference between them in the philosophy of planting. Robinson opposed the reign of exotics and the bastardized formalities that went with them, such as superimposed geometric shapes. He proposed instead that gardeners should turn to the model of plants growing in the wild. Because his influence was so great, the assumption – still current today – has arisen that all that was needed to make a beautiful garden was to choose beautiful plants and grow them in appropriate conditions. Robinson's excellence in practising what he preached obscured the fact that horticultural expertise of itself does not lead to excellence in planting design. Gertrude Jekyll, whatever her limitations and whatever the limitations we impose on her by over-idolizing her, was of the utmost importance because she injected into the subject of planting the notion that design principles were necessary. She did not use the term 'design' because she derived her principles from the arts, especially painting. To her is due in no small measure the late twentieth-century realization that even natural planting based on ecological principles needs to be thought out with an artistic eye.

Her work in partnership with the architect Sir Edwyn Lutyens (1869–1944), together with her independent commissions, led to her making more than 350 planting plans. Her influence was even greater through her many books and articles. But although people read about her own garden – especially in *Colour in the Flower Garden* – they did not always see it:

I must ask my kind readers not to take it amiss if I mention here that I cannot undertake to show it them on the spot. ... For the sake of health and reasonable enjoyment of life it is necessary to keep it quite private, and to refuse the many applications of those who offer it visits.

This introduces a further factor in today's ideas of 'great planting' – garden visiting and the direct experience of other people's plants, styles and standards, which was unthinkable fifty years ago. Before the advent of garden visiting schemes and the opening up of country estates to the public, private gardens were, indeed, private. Nonetheless, there were exceptions. Monet's garden at Giverny was visited by many and became a legend known, for example, to Gertrude Jekyll.

Selection, so much a theme in this book, is just as difficult when it comes to singling out names as when it comes to choosing plants. In this gesture towards the individuals who have contributed to later twentieth-century notions of great planting, Beatrix Farrand's name is pre-eminent in the United States. Although she published little, the facts that her major achievement, Dumbarton Oaks, passed into the hands of Harvard University and that she designed extensively for other colleges have meant that her work in the United States has remained in the public eye and it is therefore widely known.

It is also important to recognize the gardening enthusiasts whose books helped to draw attention to certain kinds of plants. In 1951, for example, Michael Haworth-Booth published *Effective Flowering Shrubs*, an excellent guide to these plants that became popular after the Second World War. This was partly because they were seen as being less labour intensive, partly too because gardeners' eyes were opened to their beauty and versatility. Nurseries such as Hillier's, Veitch's and Reuthe's played an important part in making them accessible.

The most famous enthusiasts of all were Vita Sackville-West (1892–1962) and her husband Harold Nicolson (1886–1968). They themselves were influenced by another distinguished amateur, Lawrence Johnston at Hidcote in Gloucestershire. Vita Sackville-West's journalism acquired a wide and loyal following. 'She ruled the roost from the pages of the *Observer*,' says garden writer Deborah Kellaway. 'We spoke of her as a friend.' When the Nicolsons began to open Sissinghurst to the public from the early 1950s increasing numbers of garden visitors made the pilgrimage to Kent. So potent is the spell of Sissinghurst – now beautifully preserved by the National Trust – that it sometimes seems that the English gardening scene will never awake. But what a dream! Once seen at midsummer, its wealth of old roses can never be forgotten.

The popularization of old roses has been a major feature of later twentieth-century gardening. Two names in particular are connected with the revival. Hilda Murrell sent out wonderful catalogues from her nursery, Shrewsbury Roses. Graham Stuart Thomas

Nowhere can old roses be better appreciated than at Mottisfont, Hampshire, where they are integrated into Graham Stuart Thomas's planting design.

A startling collection of grey and silver plants at Bank House, Borwick. Icy blue festuca is prominent.

published the first of his three classics on old roses in the early 1950s, and all three have recently been reissued. The fact that he then moved on to disseminate, from Sunningdale Nurseries, the catalogue that would in 1976 become *Perennial Garden Plants* is a sign both of his versatility and of the way in which such perennials were beginning to become important again. Their revival also owed much to the work of Adrian and Alan Bloom, whose catalogues as well as their nursery at Bressingham in Norfolk made them known and accessible.

Whenever a particular group of plants becomes popular in the gardening repertoire, it is generally associated with a personality, a book or a nursery, as well as the horticultural shows. The popularity after 1950 of grey- and silver-leaved plants, whose use was begun by

Gertrude Jekyll, was due in no small measure to Mrs Desmond Underwood, who both wrote a book about them and ran the nursery, Ramparts, in Colchester. Christopher Lloyd has helped us see the value of the mixed border and its plants by books such as *The Well-Tempered Garden* as well as by his nursery and garden at Great Dixter in Sussex. His influence, because of his good eye, overlaps with that of the designers.

Two mid-twentieth-century names stand out here. One is Russell Page, whose wife fortunately persuaded him to write *The Education of a Gardener* (1962). He managed to bring the criterion of simplicity centre stage, while noting how the 'luxurious horticultural "never-never land"' continued, and bemoaning the 'formal rose beds centred on a sundial, the bird baths, planted crazy paving' and other relics from the fashions of fifty years before. The other is Lanning Roper, to whom everyone interested in the subject of this book is indebted for the heavenly saying 'Elimination is as

Christopher Lloyd's mixed border at Great Dixter offers every sort of pleasure that can be had from plants – exciting yet harmonious colours, dramatic and contrasting plant forms. Spires of *Verbena bonariensis* stand in front of *Helenium* 'Moerheim Beauty'.

less is more. He would say that abstract art has influenced him here. Coming from the profession of landscape architect, Preben Jakobsen has introduced a Scandinavian gift for form. His strong design sense, backed by immense horticultural expertise, is expressed as much in his planting as in his meticulous detailing of hard materials. His contribution to *Landscape Design with Plants* in the 1970s is one of the very few attempts to consider systematically the principles involved in planting design.

Among all these influences, Beth Chatto's has been as large as any. Her ideas and vision have reached a huge public, not least through the Chelsea Flower Show exhibits with which she started carrying off gold medals in the 1970s. The displays were a revelation, offering a new notion of great planting. For instead of concentrating on the opulent individual bloom, she taught us to appreciate plant associations, where foliage and texture were as important as flowers. Her books, catalogue and talks have helped disseminate her ideas. Nowadays numerous cottage garden displays at Chelsea are a further mark of her influence, with their combinations of the kinds of plants she has helped make popular.

Her own eye for planting has been influenced by her husband Andrew Chatto's understanding of plant ecology, by the minimalist principles of Japanese flower arrangement and the vision she herself acquired from the East Anglian painter, Sir Cedric Morris (1889–1982). Thus it has come about that Morris's aesthetics of planting, which might have remained confined to the circle of his friends and students at Benton End in Suffolk, have reached out to a far wider audience. 'You have never seen anything like his planting,' the Northamptonshire gardener Valerie Finnis once commented. 'It flowed out into the meadows.' Completely breaking with the gardening orthodoxies of the 1950s, Morris's garden used many wild species, growing them in a relaxed and apparently random way, which close observers came to see had a kind of order to it.

important as planting'. His contributions to *Country Life* and his book on town gardens helped put into circulation his own high standards of planting design.

Since the 1960s John Brookes, through his books and teaching, as well as through Denmans, the garden he runs with Joyce Robinson, has tirelessly spread the message that designing with plants is an art in which

Great Planting and the Coming Millennium

In the cycles of taste that mark the history of planting, it is the natural that predominates at the end of the twentieth century. We have an inbuilt disposition to desire that which is lost, starting with Paradise, and the loss of so many natural habitats around the world makes the rediscovery, and now the re-creation, of nature particularly precious. Some of the most exciting ideas in planting are to do with this theme, which has ecological awareness at its heart.

Such a philosophy was already being developed at the turn of the century by Karl Foerster, the German gardener and researcher into plant communities. His work was carried on by Richard Hansen, director of the university gardens at Weihenstephan, and its principles were put into practice from 1983 onwards by Rosemarie Weisse at Westpark in Munich. The same philosophy is the hallmark of the gardens of Wolfgang Oehme and James van Sweden. Their book, *Bold Romantic Gardens*, has brought ecologically well-founded planting of great beauty to the attention of many. It forms a confluence with other approaches to planting in which the natural landscape, whether tawny desert or lush green hill and field, has been approached positively.

But two points need making. The first is that some of the force of the natural styles we currently love probably comes about because of the contrast with

Do these spacious and decorative plantings at Munich Westpark point the way forwards? (See page 88.)

more formal styles that remain popular. Our ideas of standards in planting are always going to work around the axis of the contrast between formal and informal, and there will always be a place for formalism. Formal, after all, implies having form, and the old formal gardens, whether they are those of the Villa Reale near Lucca in Italy or the Palais Royal in Paris will remain a fundamental inspiration. Purely in practical terms, many sites will always call out for some kind of formality in planting.

The second point is related. It is that there are always different versions of 'great', and the newer developments on which I have laid the emphasis in this book have no more prescriptive claim to the adjective than the styles that are so widely loved, revered and

imitated. In Britain many National Trust and other heritage gardens have an immense allure. Their romantic vision is deeply bound up with the past. What could be more beautiful than the gardens of Crathes Castle in July, with their blend of old yew, herbaceous borders and views of distant blue hills where the encircling woodland opens up? Such places, with their unexpectedly domestic spirit, may well inspire the visitor to try and create some touch of similar gardening at home. And what better aspiration than to create a little bit of Sissinghurst in one's backyard?

Nevertheless, when gardeners want to create something, they have to make decisions about selection, whatever style they wish to develop, and this has particular relevance to planting. Plants are somewhat like words, in that there is a great hoard of them. The gardener or designer who wants to use them well and expressively is like a writer: he or she has to choose. Guided by clear intentions as well as by instinct and

Romantic and intimate, the herbaceous borders and surrounding landscape at Crathes Castle, Grampian, speak to every visitor.

experience, we select from the available options. I am happy to discover that the same analogy occurred to Miss Jekyll herself:

Just as an un-assorted assemblage of mere words, though they may be the best words in our language, will express no thought ... so our garden plants, placed without due consideration or definite intention cannot show what they can best do for us.

In fact, in one particular kind of writing the analogy becomes even more precise. Gardens are poetic, for we aim to create coherence and harmony through the use of such devices as rhymes and rhythms among the plants, albeit in the visual medium of planting. This does, I think, clarify the way in which consciously or unconsciously the gardener sets about selecting and combining from among the great cornucopia – or dictionary – of plants.

The story of our planting, together with our sense of what is 'great' in planting, is considerably more complex than any history of garden design. A garden is a piece of artifice not to be found in nature. Nature, on the other hand, if not tampered with or destroyed by human interference, can on occasion outdo any planter. Can any gardening, however sublime, rival an alpine scree? The elegant mechanisms of natural selection, in which a plant finds an ecological niche and can survive there in fruitful interdependence with birds and insects, are capable of producing an aesthetic that human beings cannot rival.

Moreover, there is in planting, as there is not in design, something inherently democratic because cultivation of the soil is involved. This is partly a matter of the old adage, 'When Adam delved and Eve span, Who was then the gentleman?' But some other more primeval contract to do with memory is involved, of which the cottage garden, even today, is a mysterious reminder. 'It is in the art of gardening that the individual's relationship to the soil expresses itself in a manner that is intimate yet global, local yet universal.'

Plants in the wild can fall into outstanding compositions, such as the euphorbias and opuntias on this rocky Greek mountainside.

PART II
THE LIFE OF PLANTING STYLES

ABOVE: The mirror-like surface of the pond at
Denmans, Sussex, is enhanced by simple expanses of
grass beyond. A single acer stands at the water's edge.

OPPOSITE: The artist's eye: Monet gives us
nasturtiums at Giverny as though we had never
seen them before.

Gertrude Jekyll

PRINCIPLES AND PRACTICE

Gertrude Jekyll's principles of planting were excellent. One was: 'good gardening takes rank within the bounds of the fine arts.' Another was: 'no artificial planting can ever equal that of Nature.' She brought to her gardening and planting the eye of an artist and all the criteria of an artist: a close understanding of her materials, a firm grasp of composition and, most important of all, a clear purpose. She knew how much her metier required a trained eye working

Hestercombe garden, created by Edwin Lutyens and Gertrude Jekyll, combines strong architectural lines and sensuous plant detail. The combination of paving, water and simple aquatic plants in the rill is especially pleasing.

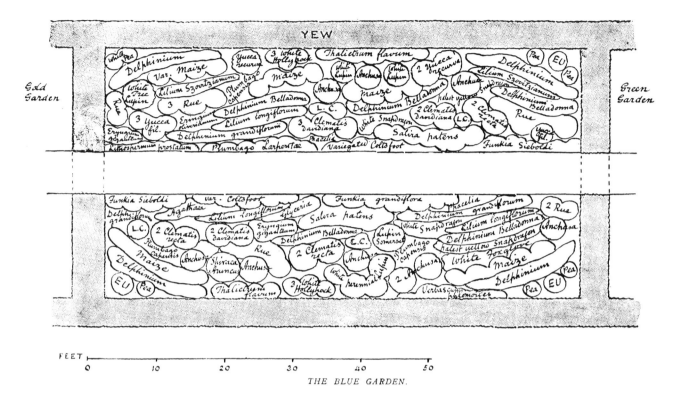

THE BLUE GARDEN.

Gertrude Jekyll's planting plan for part of her garden at Munstead Wood, Surrey, shows her bringing in touches of yellow to enhance the theme of blue.

with 'brain and heart and hand'. At the same time, the touchstone of her work was plants growing in the natural landscape. From this, she said, one may learn the great lesson: 'simplicity of intention, and directness of purpose, and the inestimable value of the quality called "breadth" in painting.'

Today her work is handed down to us in her many books, with their characteristic planting plans with the names of the plants in their little puffs of cloud. Something of the nature of her skill is still conveyed by the old black and white photographs. These can tell us much about tone and texture and a remarkable amount about plant relationships. Her planting lives, too, in a garden like Hestercombe in Somerset where the enlightened owners, the Somerset Fire Brigade, on discovering her planting plans found also the means to

restore the garden. The Jekyll look survives as well in the many gardens where her ideas have been followed, albeit using plants and hybrids that were not necessarily available in her own day.

Jekyll's gardening skills grew not from any formal training but from energetic exploration that drew on her trained talents in many crafts, including painting. She worked immensely hard, taking infinite pains over what she did. She observed cottage gardens in old Surrey, appreciating the simplicity and unpretentiousness of those 'little strips of garden' to be found by the roadside. Initially she built up a stock of plants from such places before learning that such things as plant nurseries existed. She found the ideas of William Robinson most sympathetic, became a friend and brought within the orbit of gardening his preferences: the traditions of the cottage garden as well as a feel for the wild. Her planting, it seems to me, often had a 'neat disorder' because while she was clear about her intentions, she was constantly aware of the plants themselves, what they liked and how they grew. She noted, for example, how most plants adore a long, cool root run.

Her partnership with Edwin Lutyens sharpened her sense of how gardens and plants relate to buildings they surround. The relationship poses, she says, 'a very large question'. Horticulturists tend to spoil the picture by trying to cram too much in, she says, while the architect is 'often wanting in sympathy with beautiful vegetation' – a state of affairs that is all too familiar today.

Gertrude Jekyll was a pioneer in the use of grey and silver plants. This contemporary photograph shows how skilfully she deployed them.

Gertruce Jekyll's planting was in reaction to the 'usual dreary mixture' she saw around her, the 'haphazard sprinkling of colouring without any thought of arrangement'. The bedding system favoured by so many Victorian gardeners, while 'admirable for its purpose', had managed to wreak havoc in gardens throughout the land. Yet while she acclaims the return of 'the good old garden flowers', she was pained and irritated by the lack of understanding she saw around her. Just take a clump of saxifrage in the hand, she says, and feel the way roots and stems and tufts hang together. Notice how the mind is confused by a crowded jumble and then question the confused jumble you cram into your borders.

Jekyll is a useful figure to stand at the entrance to the actual gardens in this book because, like Beatrix Farrand, she is clear about the art she practises. Her clarion cry is simplicity, both of intention and of materials: 'The very best effects are made by the simplest means, and by the use of a few different kinds of plants only at a time.' If you are planting by a stream, she says, use large drifts of water forget-me-not and meadowsweet. Where you have an old garden wall, plant it with simple plants that enjoy the habitat, such as wallflower, or even wall pennywort.

She knew that if it were to be effective, planting had to work by grouping, not by individual touches, and she constantly made notes of good companions. In the larger garden she aimed to associate large masses of plants, because by doing so you are likely to achieve cohesion. In planting a holding wall, she says, think of blocks of pattern, and then she proposes that 'it would be well to get into this kind of planting as a general rule'. And indeed her plan could well serve as the template for planting on the horizontal plane. Her metaphor for the garden is that of the picture. Planting, she says, is 'painting a landscape with living things' and the planter's 'living picture must be right from all points, and in all lights'. This metaphor seems to involve something a bit more strenuous than picturesque effects, because structure is paramount in it.

Jekyll might be regarded as interrupting what might be called an 'empire style' of planting, by which I mean planting that marches across a landscape without regard for simple and natural incidents. Her hand might be ruthless when occasion demanded, but clearly she often gardened with a gentle hand. A dry-stone wall is planted with hart's tongue fern, and other common ferns, a patch of wild campanula or a giant mullein has been allowed to seed itself, while marking the junction between the foot of the wall and some simple steps is a clump of bergenia.

Unlike Beatrix Farrand, Jekyll's work did not involve large-scale landscaping of the kind we will see

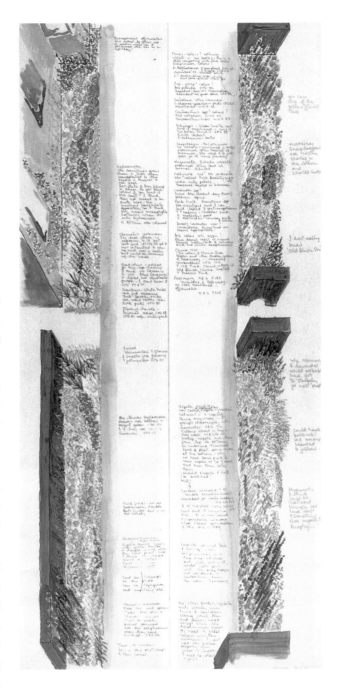

Gertrude Jekyll's reputation owes much to her restorers. This axonometric by Marian Grierson for the Rill Garden at the Deanery, Berkshire, was based on her researches of all Miss Jekyll's original (and nearly illegible) plans.

OPPOSITE: The Jekyll look seen in the purple border at Sissinghurst with softer pinks, greys and violets.

at Dumbarton Oaks (see page 34), but she had an acute sense of scale. She praises a border seen in front of a large, old and intricate dwelling, noting how appropriate are the 'bold forms of flower and leafage of peonies' in such a place. But she targets the 'petty intrusive incident' provided by the underplanting of pansies; better to have let the peonies bush over the edge of the grass. That useful device of the mowing strip, a narrow band of stone to overcome 'the tyranny of the turf edge', seems not to have occurred to her, as she then launches into a complex arrangement of men with machines and boys with bean-poles.

As for colour, in which she has been so influential, she saw that it worked best when flowers were treated as 'precious jewels in a setting of quiet environment'. This is provided in her herbaceous borders by a background of sober yew hedge or quiet wall, while grass walks act as a monochrome and fine-textured foil. Colour, as everything else in aesthetic experience, or indeed in life, works by contrast. After exposure to bright colours, she observes, the eye enjoys a rest.

What happens when a planting scheme by Jekyll is restored? Marian Grierson, who has worked on many major landscaping projects, including several of Sir Geoffrey Jellicoe's, played a large part in the restoration of the garden at the Deanery in Berkshire, a particularly successful instance of the partnership between Jekyll and Lutyens. The main garden lies on a gentle, south-facing slope. Near the house there is terracing, then what Jekyll called the Rill Garden, then another change of level leads to what was once an orchard. Many of the old trees had died by 1900, when garden works were in progress and, anticipating Sissinghurst's orchard, she grew roses over some of the survivors. A prized feature of the planting was the way

the foliage and flowers of old roses planted at the top of the terrace wall on the south side of the Rill Garden fell in great wreaths and loops, almost touching the ground below.

When she came to the Rill Garden Marian Grierson found that the structural hedges were wildly overgrown and the flower beds had crept forwards over the years. Hedges were replaced and the flower beds restored to the original depth, which meant there was a less comfortable depth for planting. But the original dimensions worked well, because the long, thin shape of the garden meant that views were unlikely to be seen face on.

Marian pored over the original plans and managed to decipher the almost illegible handwriting. She then researched the plants Gertrude Jekyll specified and was able to locate nearly all of the hybrids. To see the planting plans once she had done this reveals the quite immense labour such a planting scheme involved. To clarify the restoration enterprise to her client, Marian interpreted the planting plans in a series of three-dimensional drawings across the flowering season. The exercise demonstrated how careful and successful was Jekyll's detailing, although labour intensive to a degree that seems astonishing today.

Jekyll's borders, those she designed for clients as well as her own, show how beautifully she painted a living picture, and how sure was her colour sense. When a border is created in her spirit, as in the example taken from Sissinghurst (see page 48), the result is a confident harmony, that depends on skilled horticulture. The problem with her planting is not any lack of excellence in itself, but that it is mesmerizing and can inhibit experiment with other solutions. In particular it leaves us thinking that where there is a garden, there must be a border. Nearly one hundred years after Jekyll there must be other sorts of great planting besides borders planted in the Jekyll style!

Beatrix Farrand

EUROPEAN TIMES AMERICAN

North America's variety of plants and climates is so great it outnumbers all the kinds of gardening brought into that continent. Nonetheless, the history of gardening in North America represents a confluence of every sort of tradition. The early settlers brought their simple, modest gardens in which herbs, both medicinal and culinary, played a large part. At Monticello near Charlottesville Thomas Jefferson created an estate whose landscape aesthetics harked back to the classical values of Italy and the English eighteenth-century landscape school. Spanish settlers brought their own styles of courtyard and patio gardening.

But there is one twentieth-century figure whose work both interacts with Europe and feeds back into the Old World – Beatrix Farrand (1872–1959), a founder member of the American Society of Landscape Architects. Even more than Gertrude Jekyll, whom she greatly admired, she demonstrates just about every principle on which excellence in planting is based.

She reminds me of Edith Wharton, the novelist, who was her aunt, and had herself written a distinguished book on Italian gardens. Both women were immensely intelligent and professional in their attitudes to their work, and both came from classes more or less moneyed in which women were not expected to take up a serious job, let alone run a business. Yet Beatrix Farrand most successfully did both. I like to imagine meetings between this formidable pair when she visited her aunt in Hyères in Provence, that site of famous gardens and gardeners where Edith Wharton acquired a property on the hillside above the old town in the early 1920s – a place we will revisit later in this story. Her niece, greatly welcomed, would arrive with gifts of plants from America.

Beatrix Farrand's horticultural apprenticeship was spent under the famous curator of Boston's arboretum, Charles Singer Sargent, which helps account for her comprehensive understanding of America's native trees and the part they could play in a designed landscape. Sargent tried to keep her on the straight and narrow of horticulture, but she knew there was something more to the handling of plants and decided to go to Europe. This travel was vital, in her opinion, to the cultivation of her eye: 'It tended to form and educate the eye and train it to perceive what has been done with the opportunity given.' She looked closely at European gardens and landscape, making note and sketches. She studied old engravings of plants, which can communicate a plant's structure so vividly and so accurately. Her discriminating eye for textures, the way even two closely related sorts of box can subtly vary, is traceable to such works. Visiting England for the first time, she admired the borders at Penshurst Place, which had recently been replanted in the Jekyll style, and Vita Sackville-West's garden at Knole proved inspirational.

Later in her life she returned to England, working for Dorothy and Leonard Elmhirst at Dartington Hall in Devon. But the enterprise for which she is best remembered is Dumbarton Oaks, at Georgetown in Washington D.C. Under the enlightened patronage of Robert Woods Bliss and his wife Mildred she worked on the gardens and landscaping from 1921 to 1947. She passionately believed that if a garden were to achieve its full potential as a work of art, maintenance and active intervention were essential. The Blisses were thoroughly convinced; and, because Mildred Bliss planned to hand on the estate to Harvard University, Beatrix Farrand was persuaded in 1942 to write her 'Plant Book' for Dumbarton Oaks. This outstanding

The Villa Lante garden in Italy is both classically calm and immensely resourceful; it was a strong influence on the eye of Beatrix Farrand.

document records what she had done and what plants she used, and with sometimes uncanny accuracy projects what will be needed in the future. The University was able to supply competent maintenance, with the result that, on the whole, Dumbarton Oaks continues to represent her intentions.

Arriving at Dumbarton Oaks, Farrand was, in the words of Mrs Bliss, 'attentive to the light and wind and grade [slope] of each area'. The end result was to be a landscape of discrete and usually enclosed garden areas, with a subtle flow between them, moving from formality near the house to more informal naturalistic planting further off. The site's natural topography always came first with the 'landscape gardener', as Farrand called herself. The gardens were arranged around it 'with as little dislocation as was reasonably possible'. In the famous Forsythia Plantation, which covers an extremely steep bank, she saw the modelling of the hillside as an essential part of its beauty. Today the annual pruning she recommended is too expensive, and it has become what she feared, 'only a tangled, even if lovely, group of planting'.

Similarly she aimed to preserve and display in the best possible way the magnificent black oaks and other native trees she found when she arrived. 'Towering oaks and beeches were left undisturbed, therefore they have not suffered as changes of level were made beyond the spread of their roots and branches.' This policy accounts, for example, for the slightly unusual shape and dimensions of the Beech Terrace. She was keenly aware that even fine trees 'do not show up for much' if 'they are not led up to in any way'. Consequently nothing distracts from the single beech tree here (a 1950s replacement of the original). Elsewhere, trees that were outstanding features in 1921, such as a Katsura tree (*Cercidiphyllum japonicum*) and a fine *Acer palmatum*, are still the focus of a long view, whereas less thoughtful garden planting would long ago have obscured them.

I dwell on the trees because they are truly such a crucial element in the greatness of her planting and

OPPOSITE: The lucid design and harmony here, especially between the hard materials and the planting, are a good example of the European heritage that Beatrix Farrand assimilated into her own style.
BELOW: Beatrix Farrand thought spatially and provided superb detailing, such as this path and its relation to planting and columns demonstrate.

The Katsura tree, *Cercidiphyllum japonicum*, valued by Beatrix Farrand for its shape and canopy, is a treasure that is under-appreciated by today's designer. A venerable specimen is to be found at Sezincote, Gloucestershire, where it has what it likes: a generous water supply. Just before the leaves fall, you will smell strawberries as you pass by.

vistas, as in the sloping alley of old silver maples in the upper part of Melisande's Alley. She saw how, near the house, they could provide an outside green room, and how the music room, with the Copse brought up close to it, might seem to be part of the surrounding woods. (Visitors to Glasgow's Burrell Art Gallery can enjoy a similarly magic sensation, for in the glass-clad back of the building, you seem to be embraced by the trees outside.) Elms alongside evergreens at the edge of the property were planted to provide screening, and this is a work of art in its own right.

She scrupulously studied the textures of trees, both of bark and foliage. Conifers were banned from the garden below the main entrance because she thought that their foliage would not harmonize with the fine textures of box, yew and pyracantha. By the east wall of the Fountain Terrace, she planted a row of Kieffer pears 'as a support to the garden, which otherwise would be obviously hanging over retreating grades [slopes] and suspended unpleasantly in the air'. She planted one hillside with single-flowering cherries, recommending that as they came to the end of their natural life they should be replaced with a variety such as *Prunus* x *subhirtella* 'Autumnalis', rather than more hybridized kinds. Another hillside she painted with crabapples, using just a few varieties. By the oval Lovers' Lane pool, she planted a single silver acer, which would be reflected in the water, so that the physical matter of trees becomes an abstract study in branching lines. Her skill in deploying trees gives an extra dimension to the notion of great planting.

Her plant palette was remarkably small. She used the same modest native plants again and again, thereby

carry out her design exceptionally well. She revealed their sculptural qualities, realizing, like Gertrude Jekyll, that their structure in winter could be as beautiful as their summer colour. She used them to create

creating harmonies that run across the site. Yet the ways in which she used them undergo endless variation. Take box. A pair of *Buxus sempervirens* 'Suffruticosa' figured as accent plants by the orangery door. Simple symmetry turns into a more subtle form of balance when one of them is flanked by the type species, *B. sempervirens*. Elsewhere, waves of trimmed box run either side of a curving path, where their simplicity is matched by the simple basket weave pattern of the brick. In the Box Walk it is used in a more ceremonial way, while throughout the garden, such plantings of box interact with and show off beautiful detailing in bench, floor and wall. Again, *Vinca minor* is a plant she uses repeatedly, but her list of ground-cover plants includes choices less familiar today, like the elegant *Fragaria chiloensis*.

She was keenly aware of the importance of contrasts and of developing the individual character of each part of the garden. Appropriateness is the key to her planting. 'If bulbs are used in the Green Garden they should be of quite different sorts from those used elsewhere ... as the Green Garden has a quality of its own which should be emphasized by planting.' So she recommended jonquils, 'of the single campernelle sorts', the small *Narcissus poeticus* and white crocus. Looking at my own garden in the light of this advice, I now see what needs to be done!

Beatrix Farrand thought that structure and form came before colour in a garden. The preference is part of her understatement, whose eloquence is easily missed in a late twentieth-century horticultural world abounding with the seductive colours of new hybrids. Nevertheless, she intended bold colour statements at Dumbarton Oaks, even if she confined the flowery part of the garden to terraces on the east side of the house. She wanted the Rose Garden to progress from pink and salmon colouring in the southern third, through salmon-coloured and yellowish-pink roses, to 'yellow or predominantly yellow sorts' in the northern third. At the same time, to meet her clients' wishes and

because she knew that the garden would be seen a lot in winter when ownership of it was transferred to Harvard, she designed it to be as interesting in winter as in summer. More box! The central plant could be allowed to grow quite high, she said. Admitting that the box bushes she used for accents were bad neighbours for roses, she nonetheless allowed the 'structural and aesthetic virtue' of these evergreens to prevail.

The herbaceous borders that flourished in the 1930s were too expensive to maintain as Farrand wanted them. But let us look as though through her own eyes, taking in the whole aspect of this part of the gardens: 'since the Fountain Terrace has usually been adapted to the orange, yellow, bronze, and maroon shades, it has seemed natural, during the spring and summer months, to give the shades of pink, red, lavender, and pale blue to the range of the Herbaceous Border.'

To what extent were her colour tastes ours, and to what extent was she, like us, either fallible or trapped in tastes of her time? The Cherry Hill comes into flower at the same time as the Forsythia Plantation below. This strikes me as a misjudgement. Not because pink and yellow must never be mixed for, as Christopher Lloyd maintains, certain sorts of pink and yellow make exciting, even harmonious neighbours; but the strong, even aggressive yellow of forsythia is not a felicitous neighbour to the delicate pink of cherry blossom. As for the colours of the roses she used, taste has moved away from them, and they have even been described as rather brash.

One of the best tributes I know to Dumbarton Oaks, aside from the pleasure it gives to its visitors, is that Lanning Roper paid it long and lingering visits. I think if one wants an example of plants used as the instruments of design, of planting that deals in, as Gertrude Jekyll would say, the large effects as well as 'lesser beautiful incidents', of planting done with the utmost attention to scale, there could be no better living picture.

The Cottage Garden

There are several schools of thought concerning the cottage garden. For some people it represents romanticism at large: the urban dweller's nostalgic dream for an illusory rural past. For such people the cottage garden is a species of the seductive picturesque and a betrayal of the conditions of actual poverty endured by cottagers over the centuries. Other people see it as the garden that, *par excellence*, speaks to the heart, with its unaffected random mixture of annuals, perennials, roses, a few fruit trees and, perhaps, some rows of vegetables. For clear-minded designers, the cottage garden is simply the enduring informal style. Versions of formality come and go – parterre, carpet bedding, modernist geometry – but the cottage garden endures.

Its history can be used to prove the validity of all these points of view. The former tenants of one cottage garden I know are recorded in an aged sepia photograph. They are standing by the front door of the small, primitive dwelling, and few luxuries in the way of plants are visible in their garden. As recently as the 1960s their only water supply was a pump at the foot of the garden. No wonder cottagers have been known to flee to newer houses and better standards of living. But the little house still stands, surviving against all the odds over several centuries and scarcely changed over the last thirty years. It fits so snugly into a fold of the hillside that you can go down the lane without noticing its existence. There have been thousands of other comparable meek dwellings. One way to do justice to their spirit of survival seems to be to give them the

BELOW: A traditional mix of flowers and vegetables in a cottage garden: cabbage, lobelia and calendula.

garden style that harmonizes with them, and that echoes, however faintly, their past.

Even for those who do not live in cottages, nor in the countryside, the cottage garden style in the late twentieth century, an era that has managed to spawn so many hostile environments, is likely to be popular. For the cottage garden is about feeling at home. Its homely message is produced by the scale which, as of the cottage itself, is modest and ordinary. Typically, both dwelling and garden belong to each other and to their landscape. Many traditional cottage garden plants are unhybridized and closely related to wild flowers, as well as having been grown in gardens for centuries. No wonder the planting style translates so well, when it is all about belonging; although, needless to say, it will look inappropriate if it is made the adjunct to a grand or formal or austerely modernist building.

Lanning Roper was thinking about writing a book on cottage garden plants, when he discovered that Margery Fish, whose own garden at East Lambrook Manor in Somerset was an inventive variation on the cottager's, had pipped him at the post. *Cottage Garden Flowers* (1960) is still a wonderful way into the plants to use. When she wrote it, Margery Fish lamented the widespread mindless destruction of the old dwellings that had occurred in her lifetime. She also noted how the old flowers that the cottager had cherished for so many years were 'finding their way back to the larger gardens'. She played no small part in this process, through her books, her plant nursery and through opening her garden to visitors. Margery Fish is, in fact, the major figure in the revival of the cottage garden that has been with us since the 1960s. In her book, astrantias, which are now to be found in many nursery catalogues, received a chapter to themselves. She directed her readers back to the virtues of primroses, fumitory, southernwood (*Artemisia abrotanum*), pulmonarias and soapwort (*Saponaria officinalis*). This 'real cottage garden plant', she reminds us, fully justifies its name, for it can be used to wash old and delicate fab-

When it comes to colour, Monet is not the only one to know how to make an impact. This exuberant spring planting creates a quilt that is typical of the cottage-garden style.

rics. Like Gertrude Jekyll, she knew what an excellent plant was *Francoa ramosa*, the bridal wreath, even if it needed protection in winter. And also, like Jekyll, she saw how well the elder, *Sambucus nigra*, went with modest old buildings and their gardens. The elder was loved and admired by John Constable, who likened its creamy flowers to scrambled eggs. It is a hedgerow plant throughout the British Isles, and it strikes the note of ordinariness that runs through many cottage gardens. But it is precisely in the ordinary that the greatness of cottage gardens resides.

Hudson's

The cottage I referred to on page 41 is called Hudson's. It is in East Anglia and has a quintessential cottage garden. Everything on the 1,350 sq m (one-third of an acre) patch of ground is all of a piece, whether you look at how unselfconsciously it is grafted into the landscape, or at how, in the house, an ancient and paint-scarred door hangs crookedly but securely on its original hinges.

The path leads, as it should, from front gate to front door. To one side is a little round bed, which glows with mixed wallflowers in spring and again in summer with simple dahlias, in clear shades of red, white, yellow and one or two oranges. Mixed in is one sophisticate, the Bishop (*Dahlia* 'Bishop of Llandaff'), whose small vermilion flowers flame on foliage that can look almost black. This brings a touch of intensity to the group.

On the other side of the path is a long bed, about 5.5m (18ft) long by 1.2m (4ft) deep, and behind it are the remains of an ancient cherry tree. In the old photograph it is still alive, but now it is simply a skeleton that props up climbing rose 'Albertine'. The bed was there when the owners arrived, although smaller, and with little in it but a big patch of pale blue Michaelmas daisies and *Aconitum napellus* var. *napellus* (syn. *A. anglicum*), which is, as its early name suggests, native to Britain. In the patch of meadow behind the bed grows wild soapwort that is allowed now and again into the cultivated

quilt of flowers. It looks as though it has a family resemblance to the phloxes that grow at the back of the bed (although it is, in fact, unrelated). Some of these phloxes came, unnamed, from a local farm where they had grown over generations. *Cichorium intybus* (wild chicory), which grows in the grass, has recently found its way into the border, and it is properly valued for its startlingly clear but slightly chalky blue flowers borne on tall stems.

Sheila, the gardener, has acquired whatever flowers she liked the look of, but always with an eye to how they might blend in. *Chelone obliqua*, from North America, is just right among phlox and tradescantia, and *Gaura lindheimeri*, a comparatively recent introduction to British gardens, fits in perfectly because it is simple and unhybridized. It is the sort of modest flower one would expect to find by the roadside.

Height is carefully considered, which is one reason the bed looks so good. Also, although the colours are not planned rigorously, the planting is anything but spotty because many plants are repeated. Choices are attuned to one another and the general effect is soft, although penstemons provide colour brilliance here and there. If one way of visualizing flowers is as a quilt, another is as a woven fabric which, as you gaze at it, reveals many layers.

Pale yellow and chalky pink hollyhocks stand either

The quilt-like bed at Hudson's, 5.5 x 1.2m (18 x 4 ft).

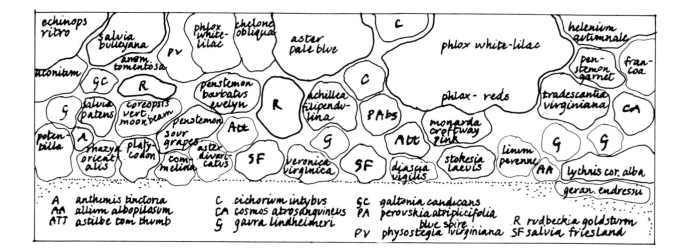

grass and hedge, and the steep rabbity hillside on the far side of the lane. The cottage and its garden are distinct, but never that far away from melting back into the landscape from which they arose.

LEFT: Familiar and well-loved plants, such as lavender and digitalis (foxglove), create a garden that is in harmony with the surrounding countryside in a cottage garden at Boxford in Suffolk.
BELOW: Drifts of calendula team up in the most natural way possible with the brick of the house at Upper Woodhill Farm, Surrey.

side of the front door. These just stay around, seeding themselves here and there in the position that all hollyhocks seem to love, close up against the wall of the house where there is warmth and reflected light. Hybrid tea roses are anathema in the garden. Instead, *Rosa* 'Mme Alfred Carrière' grows to one side of the door and further along is a great rose 'Félicité et Perpétue', which was already there when the owners arrived. *Artemisia* 'Powis Castle' stands in for the *A. abrotanum* that is synonymous with a cottage garden. It is joined, growing in front of the house, by *Fuchsia magellanica*, another plant that predates the present regime.

This garden is hard work, for the local soil is sandy and needs to have a lot of compost dug into it each autumn. Perhaps because the soil is dry and not rich, few of the plants spread themselves, a sign also that they 'enjoy each other's company', as Margery Fish put it, and are in balance with each other. Some plants are difficult, such as the big hybridized clematis, however much the soil is composted. This failure is appropriate, for in the small enclosure, whose boundary hedges are made up of thorn and plum, holly, hazel and stretches of lilac, the cultivated clematis would be too exotic. Looking across the flower bed, the view is to meadow,

Waveney Rising

Waveney Rising, Deborah and Bill Kellaway's garden near Diss, Norfolk, covers about 0.4 hectares (1 acre). It lies around and to the south of their thatched cottage and slopes gently down to the watery meadows that edge the River Waveney at its source. They created the garden, even down to the hedges, in the years following 1965. When they arrived, virtually its only feature was a kidney-shaped flower bed, barely visible through the rough long grass and brambles. Now it is most distinctly a cottage garden in feel, although it is far larger

Originally kidney-shaped, this bed of 'coloured hay' is now aligned with the yew hedges beyond and fits perfectly into the overall scheme.

than the type, and contains elements that are just as distinctly not cottagey. There is the slightly surreal feature of a square bracket of yew hedge filled in with clipped shrubs and flowers and a seat. There are many metres of yew hedges, which you might imagine would give the garden the character of formality; but they do not. From the front door (which in the Kellaway's occupancy has become topographically the back door) runs a bold diagonal axis, giving a view to the river meadow. These came from conscious design decisions, but they do not interfere with the unselfconscious air of the rest of the garden.

The Kellaways have not restored a cottage garden, and, if there is such a thing as a formula for a cottage garden, they have not followed it. Instead, they have interpreted the spirit of such a garden, always with

The old front door is framed by apple trees, underplanted with traditional cottage garden plants, such as valerian and old roses.

clear intentions in mind. They found their guide in Russell Page, who explains, persuasively, that the garden maker needs to decide on a governing idea that is in keeping with the character of the plot. This character they took from 'the large quiet spaces of the landscape', and the decision moulded all their thinking, even though plans were never drawn.

They achieved their aims in several simple, clear ways. For a start they planted native trees, such as poplar, hazel, willow and yew, and created hedges out of time-honoured species such as hornbeam and holly and beech. Their fruit trees were apple and cherry and pear. Such choices wedded the garden both to the local landscape and to tradition.

Then they simplified the original kidney-shaped bed and lined it up with a newly planted yew hedge, with the result that its new, long rectangular shape fell into

place, and now coheres in a larger scheme. This bed had been planted by Adrian Bloom in the 1950s; fortunately for Waveney Rising, the nurseries of Bloom's of Bressingham are close by. Alan Bloom has been a pioneer in reintroducing good old herbaceous plants, and he had used plants like achillea, whose wild relative, yarrow, is widely distributed in Britain, and monkshood, again a plant with native relations. These go in for a bit of seeding, and are strong enough not to need staking, provided you do not mind a slightly casual look. After all, Russell Page points out, herbaceous plants are basically meadow plants, and what is the look of a good border but coloured hay? This made

Cottage-garden style herbs look at home against a backcloth of formal yew hedges. *Salvia sclarea* var. *turkestanica* is the star here. Earlier, angelica is the diva.

were joined by heleniums, japanese anemones, sedums and the great silvery flaggy forms of the globe thistle, *Echinops ritro*, and cardoon, looking at home in the local landscape. Cow parsley, which is encouraged all around the boundaries of the garden, is firmly kept out here. As for that hayfield, they cut and cut and cut it, until eventually they had a lawn. Grass is, in fact, an uncottagey feature, but there is something about Waveney Rising's grass that tells you it once belonged to a field, and for that, or some other, reason it is perfectly right and proper.

Two features directly derive from cottage gardens: a garden path leading away from the front door (that has become the back door), and a herb patch by the back door (that has become the main entrance). The garden path they flanked by symmetrical lines of apple trees. Under them they grew plants such as *Iris foetidissima* and ajuga and white honesty. Gradually they developed two borders. Although these run in parallel with the 'coloured hay' border, and in a sense gesture towards it, they are planted with more traditional cottage garden plants: auriculas, dicentras, phlox, *Alchemilla mollis*, delphiniums, peonies and shrub roses. A branch of *Rosa moyesii* eventually joined up with an apple bough from across the path to form a natural arch. *R. moyesii* is a good example of using a plant that is not strictly speaking from the cottage's repertoire but is the right character and so falls happily into place.

The 'herby bit' by the entrance is the core of the garden's feeling. It evolved slowly, and on little money. A single area of paving was created out of pamments, the local square flooring brick. When the need emerged, and funds allowed, the pamments were extended, so that there is now a practical space for a small table and benches. The herbs and flowers here are so eloquent partly because you sit among them, as well as brush past them to reach the door, and look out of the kitchen window over them to the slightly formal *allée* beyond. The flower that stands out is the biennial

good sense to the Kellaways since they had initially glimpsed Alan Bloom's plants struggling through the virtual hayfield that was the 'garden' they had acquired. Over the years these herbaceous perennials

Salvia sclarea var. *turkestanica*, which Deborah Kellaway originally grew from a packet of seeds. Its offspring she lets be or moves around the space, depending where they appear. The soft crinkled fudginess of its green leaves with a trace of grey shows up against the yew hedge at the side and contrasts with the smart visual order of the leaves of agapanthus, grown in pots.

There are all the herbs you would hope to find in such a place: borage, lovage, fennel, lad's love or southernwood, chives (or at least alliums), golden origanum, rosemary, thyme and rue. The tall flowers of angelica are positively voluptuous in summer, seen against dark yew. There is a supporting cast of grey-leaved plants like santolinas, lavender, the curry plant (*Helichrysum italicum*) and a rose or two. One is the apothecary's rose, *R. gallica* var. *officinalis*; the other is the old china rose, *R.* x *odorata* 'Mutabilis', again a plant not strictly of cottage gardens but so simple, for all that its flowers change from peach to a deep pink, that it looks perfectly at home. There are some exotics too, like *Nectaroscordum siculum* ssp. *bulgaricum* (formerly *Allium bulgaricum*); but because of its perceptible relation to chives it is quite in keeping. The lay-out of this area is all done by eye, deliberately avoiding an arithmetical symmetry, but looking for a harmonious balance. Details of the planting change year by year, for the sandy soil and high light level encourage seeding, but the structural elements, both in planting and paving, ensure that with weeding and judicious elimination the identity of the place is constant. A feature of this bit of the garden are several not so little box bushes, kept trimmed into spheres; they were bought locally and inexpensively, and then the Kellaways looked long and carefully before deciding where they should go.

In a way this careful looking is the secret of their garden, because it leads to such judicious choices. Where the garden edges the watery meadows by the river, there is now a post and rail fence, and a picket

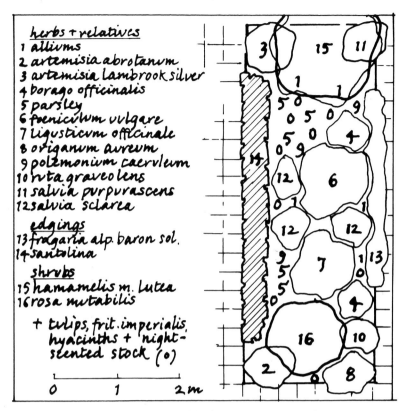

Abundance is the keynote of this herb bed at Waveney Rising. The paving is of pamments, a local square flooring brick.

gate in it. The planting next to it consists of tree lupins, euphorbias, a golden elder and a fastigiate beech. Such planting is not literally to be found in the next hedgerow, but it has links with local versions, while providing more visual excitement.

The best picture of the garden is given by Deborah's book about it, *The Making of a Country Garden* (1988), because she explains all the judging of things by eye that went on before decisions were taken, so the reader gains a clear sense of how a lay-out, most coherent in its end result, gradually evolved. The book also gives some idea of the consistent hard work that went on over years – and still goes on – for all this to be achieved.

The Cottage Garden, Sissinghurst

In this famous garden, Vita Sackville-West and Harold Nicolson took a traditional style and transformed it so that although the place is totally recognizable as a cottage garden, the effect is quite new.

The front of the cottage is demure old brick, worn and rich in texture. The rose covering it is a tranquil old favourite, *Rosa* 'Madame Alfred Carrière', with creamy white, sweet-smelling flowers in early summer and a second flowering later. Windows either side of the little front door are leaded and speak of the past. The garden paths are indeed appropriately made of pieces of old stone and brick, in the quietest fashion, and divide the area into four quadrants. There is a feeling of enclosure that is quite traditional. Many of the plants too are cottage kinds, whatever the season: tulips, pansies, columbines, iris, lupins, pinks, nasturtiums, snapdragons, *Thunbergia alata* (black-eyed Susan), achilleas and crocosmias. Four fastigiate yews (planted in 1934), also cottagey in associations, are grouped around the big old copper container at the centre. These are simple elements; there is not a phormium or a yucca in sight.

And yet one is in another country. The reason is, of course, the colour range. What happened here was that the Nicolsons – and Harold in particular – brought to bear on a cottage garden the idea of a restricted range of colour. But instead of using understatement and emotional restraint, this planting flaunts the dangerous range of red, yellow and orange. The nearest that blue can get to this garden is within the faded red of a columbine. The nearest white comes to it is in the blossoms of *Rosa* 'Madame Alfred Carrière'. The reds stray scarcely at all beyond vermilion, and have nothing to do with pinks and magentas. Shrubs and small trees towards the bounding hedges are yellow, such as

Warm colours – of aquilegias and lupins – press upon the visitor from all sides in the Cottage Garden at Sissinghurst.

an elaeagnus and a Mount Etna broom, *Genista aetnensis*.

The effect is extraordinary. There is no escape into soft greys as a way out of the experience. A sharp silver, such as that of *Artemisia ludoviciana*, only serves to accentuate the intensity of an adjacent patch of orange. Gentle variegated leaves, such as those of felicia to be found in pots on the steps below the tower, are absent. The varieties of green in this garden are startling, and can be a little sinister, beginning with the incisive verdigris patina of the old copper container that sits at the centre, and its almost violent contrast with the black green of the four yews, brought out by the orange *Mimulus aurantiacus* (syn. *M. glutinosus*) with which it is planted in summer The foliage of the great mounds of *Euphorbia griffithii* 'Fireglow' is the curious browny tinge of green that indicates the presence of its complementary colour, red. The well-marshalled leaves of *Crocosmia* 'Lucifer' look as ever all the greener for being cheek by jowl with hot, red flowers, and especially so in a setting that keeps up

the insistence on both green and red. Often, too, the green hints at black, as in the foliage of veratrum and lilies that shoot and billow up in early summer. Some of the pressure of colour here is taken away by yellow achilleas and day-lilies, but the cultivars tend to weightiness, rather than offering pale sulphurs and chalky lemon yellows.

An interesting foliage colour comparison can be made with the red border at Hidcote, in Gloucestershire. Here there are many of the same flame red flowers, but next to them is the deep burgundy of *Cordyline australis* 'Purpurea', whose leaf shape is not dissimilar to that of crocosmia. But the Cottage Garden at Sissinghurst has nothing to do with

OPPOSITE: The flat plates of achillea and trim horizontals of yew hedges are in play with verticals: verbascums, *Thalictrum flavum* ssp. *glaucum*, iris leaves and (right) a yew tree.
BELOW: A traditional cottage, traditional yews, but a cottage-garden style transformed by Harold Nicolson's strong colour preferences.

OPPOSITE: Orange cheiranthus are boldly brought in to raise the temperature of planting at the foot of the wall. The climbing rose, beautifully pruned and trained, is *R.* 'Madame Alfred Carrière'.

Australasian exotics, nor with the crimson and pinks that lie towards blue in the spectrum and that would break out of the web of yellow, red and green. At Sissinghurst the planting is loaded towards the familiar, and yet by an insistence on a narrow, intense colour range, transforms the order of experience.

The force of the planting statement in this cottage garden is emphasized by shapes and lines. The four erect little yews and the crocosmia's swords are opposed by insistent horizontals from many achilleas and the tops of hedges trimmed with knife-edge precision. Such Mondrian-like oppositions are played off against arcs and curves. Everything is distinct, everything is close and there are no misty blues and hazy violets to give us distance, by appearing to recede behind warmer colours; and of course, because the garden is enclosed, there are no long axial vistas – unless you peer through the round hole that was created a few years ago in the yew hedge leading to the rose garden.

For a long time when I visited this garden I did not photograph it or make a note of what plants were in it, although, along with countless other garden enthusiasts, I did so elsewhere in the garden. After all, I told myself, there was no way I could grow such sun-lovers in my town garden with its shade from buildings and trees, so what was the point of looking too closely? But my reaction involved something more. The hot colours of the small enclosed garden are intensely emotional. When Vita Sackville-West would have been happy to allow in television in the early 1950s, Harold Nicolson put his foot down: it would be 'exposing my intimate affections to the public gaze'. Is it in order for the visitor to remain at ease with the strong feeling displayed, especially when Gertrude Jekyll herself had said that 'flame reds and oranges excite us too much and must

be used very sparingly'? The garden here jettisons colours associated with social correctness. It is a part of Sissinghurst where Jekyll's sort of reticence is dismissed. It signals the Nicolsons' decision to live rather more dangerously, dismissing the pallid tints of conventional British society at the time.

Of course, with an estate the size of Sissinghurst you could always find somewhere else to cool off, and the Cottage Garden's effectiveness depends on its sheer difference. If you have only a pocket-sized patch to call your own, red and yellow are a fairly desperate option. But, given the Nicolsons' means, what stylish achievement, to marry the homeliness of the real cottage garden with a vision so much stronger and assertive! And how much it meant to visitors when they started arriving in the early 1950s. Like Elizabeth David's *Mediterranean Food* (1950), written as an antidote to the 'bleak conditions' of post-war Britain, Sissinghurst put an exotic warmth and colour within the reach of anyone who wanted to emulate such colour cookery.

A plan of the gardens at Sissinghurst showing the Cottage Garden on the right and, on the left, the White Garden (see page 103).

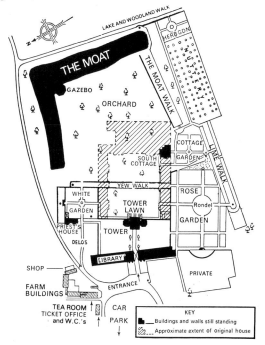

The Artist's Eye

MONET AT GIVERNY, SHEILA JACKSON IN LONDON, DEREK JARMAN AT DUNGENESS

By the nature of their profession artists take visual risks and break rules. So, when they make gardens, they can surprise and inspire us by making what cannot be found in any book or anywhere before in the history of gardening. When they are interested in plants, they often use them with great originality because their habitual employment of a visual language enables them to make connections and find visual solutions that are unlikely to be within the reach of those of us who are less visually literate. A painter learns to see the visual relationships between things. At a drawing or painting class, the tutor may say: 'Forget you are looking at a nose, a neck, a hand, a shoulder,

Irises by Sir Cedric Morris. Irises appeal to painters because of their strong forms and clear colours.

A giant bronze head at Stoneypath, where sculptures and plants combine to create overtones of temples and politics.

and think instead about these familiar items as shapes and colours, and how they relate to what is next to them.' Painters and sculptors train their eye to see the world not just literally – 'that is a fern, that is a stone, that is a pond' – but to observe how all the visual qualities of these things connect. They often see a plant as an abstract form. The point about this way of looking is that it goes hand in hand with the aim of creating a coherent picture, a cohesive composition. And that is precisely what – in three dimensions, or rather in four, because in gardens there is always the element of time – the garden maker is doing.

John Nash (1893–1977), brother of Paul Nash, called himself an 'artist plantsman'. He was a painter, mainly of landscapes, a fine botanical illustrator and an excellent gardener. Artists such as Nash tend to like plants with a clear structure, for the simple reason that they are more rewarding to paint. Think of Monet's irises, or of those beauties – and sometimes monsters – that Georgia O'Keeffe saw as if through binoculars, huge scale! Insight provided by their drawings or paintings can give us a clearer idea of how to make the most of the plant's qualities in the garden, either in relation to other plants, or to stone or brick, or to the landscape. Paintings can, in short, help give us a trained eye, that recurrent aim of 'great planters' from end to end of the twentieth century.

I have for the moment laid the stress on structure because, for the last few decades, it has seemed to many thoughtful and successful gardeners that gardens are primarily spatial structures, rather like sculptures in a beautiful gallery, where both the sculptures and the surrounding room are created by plants and their adjuncts, the 'hard landscaping'. And it so happens that many beautiful artists' gardens in the second half of the twentieth century, like that made by Sue and Ian Hamilton Finlay at Stoneypath in Scotland, involve sculpture and are spatially moving experiences.

But what touches the feelings with the greatest immediacy is colour. Exciting colour in a garden can make life glow, and of course the artist's garden that made us all realize what wonderful places artists' gardens could be is that of the great colourist, Claude Monet. He is only an eye, said Cézanne; 'but my God what an eye!'

Monet at Giverny

Claude Monet (1840–1926) rented the pink house and its 1 hectare (2½ acre) walled garden, called the Clos Normand, from 1883. He wanted a home for a joint family: his two children and himself, now widowed, and Alice de Hoschedé and her six children, abandoned as an act of desperation by her bankrupted husband, the businessman and collector of pictures and talent, Ernest Hoschedé. Monet developed the garden with increasing intensity from then on.

First, he and his gardeners worked on the enclosed garden. Here his originality can be gauged by looking at the design advice given by Joseph Decaisne and Charles Naudin in the well-known *Manuel de l'amateur des jardins*, which was published in four volumes in 1860–72; he is said to have owned a copy of this work. Decaisne and Naudin give the excellent advice to avoid 'confusion of styles by indiscriminate planting', but when it comes to the lay-out for a 'landscape garden of small size, comprising from five to ten acres [2–4 hectares]' they provide a plan that looks like a park, with an ellipse of drives and connecting curlicues of smaller paths. In the middle of the ellipse lies a lake with an island. The planting they envisage is of trees and shrubs. Interestingly, when Monet came to construct his lily ponds the shapes he chose and winding paths were not dissimilar to Decaisne and Naudin's model. But, encouraged by the painter Gustave Caillebotte (1848–94), he laid out the Clos Normand in the style of the vegetable garden to be glimpsed at the lower right corner of their plan. This was practical and necessary, of course; there were many mouths to be fed and little money, so the household needed to grow their own fruit and vegetables. But the point of this market garden lay-out (as an early visitor with some surprise recognized it to be) was that the principle crop should be flowers: flowers to be cut and

Informal bedding of tulips and myosotis at Giverny. Harmony between the house colour and nearby planting was of great importance to Monet.

Here iris flowers look like so many dabs of colour in one of Monet's paintings. The limestone hills, glimpsed beyond the house, are of great importance in framing this part of the garden.

painted, when the weather prevented Monet from painting outside, and flowers as a spectacle on a scale that filled the whole field of vision. Walls, trees and vertical features, such as metal arches, and the mass of the pink house hold them in place.

Monet took a well-known idea, the flower garden, in the sense of flowers for cutting, and pushed it as far as it would go. This was part of the garden's genius. Another part of this was the simplicity of the plan, which rather resembles today's tubs of paint in a water-colour box: quantities of little rectangular flower-beds filling the spaces provided by a grid of narrow paths. These are laid out, along with grass areas, on either side of the wide central alley, the *grande allée*, which was in the garden when Monet took it over. So in the bare lay-out – and perhaps in winter, when Monet was living elsewhere – there are a lot of straight lines. As the growing season progresses, this grid vanishes under flowers, grown in flower beds in which, follow-ing the practice of the time, the well-composted soil was built up several inches. This has the result of increasing height down the middle of the bed, and making a strong contrast with the lowest edges, by the paths. In 1904 a visitor said: 'the profusion – this teeming aspect ... gives the garden a special quality.' Today it is precisely this aspect that is still so impres-sive. Planting is so dense the paths become invisible, and one is only aware of wave after wave of flowers.

As for the kinds and combinations of plants that Monet grew, the style is actually like that of the cottage garden, although the order of experience is different

OPPOSITE: Alongside Giverny's teeming profusion there are broad, simple gestures such as in this helianthus-lined path.

because of the scale. The plants on the whole are simple: poppies, peonies, cornflowers. The apotheosis of simplicity occurs in the *grande allée* where, under the metal arches that carry midsummer's roses, nasturtiums edge inwards from the sides until by late summer only a small path winds between the adventuring stems and flowers. Monet shows us nasturtiums as though we had never seen them before. Decaisne and Naudin talk about how a garden should have its 'appropriate magnificence', but I do not think that anyone at that time could have imagined the magnificence of simplicity in this way, especially in an era when bedding out was still popular. Actually, Monet did some bedding out himself, in the flower beds that run parallel to the front of the house. This planting works wonderfully in the spring, with tulips standing above forget-me-nots, but the later season's scheme of hundreds of pelargoniums has a contrivance that is alien to the cottage flowers in the main part of the garden.

Monet, of course, also grew hundreds of irises, in great patches and rows of a single colour. They lie alongside herbaceous plantings so that although in late May they are the chief spectacle, they are never seen in isolation. When they finish flowering, other flowers take over. In some parts of the garden, lines of irises lead the eye towards the limestone hills that run behind and parallel to the house. These hills are rarely remarked in accounts of the garden, but their presence is an integral part of the atmosphere of the place, as important as the poplars and watery realms of the river at the other end of the little estate.

Today, while colour is the garden's chief impact, it is hard to discern a system or indeed to imagine that a precise colour system, beyond anything indicated in some of Monet's paintings of the gardens, ever prevailed. Monet, like other painters of his time, was influenced by the colour theories of Michel Eugène

Monet took care to keep the water clear between the clumps of water-lilies to maximize reflections of the sky in the water's surface. Originally the banks around the pond were of grass, a happier solution than the planting used today to protect the pond edge from visitors.

Chevreul (1786–1889). So there is a constant play on what are called complementary colours. These pairs of colours, as the English garden writer and photographer Andrew Lawson (who is himself a painter) explains 'provide the maximum available contrast. Nothing could be less purple than yellow. Green is the furthest one can go from red.' Such colours, used judiciously, can enhance and animate each other. You do not want equal amounts of each colour in the pair next to one another; in such an arrangement they fight. But the

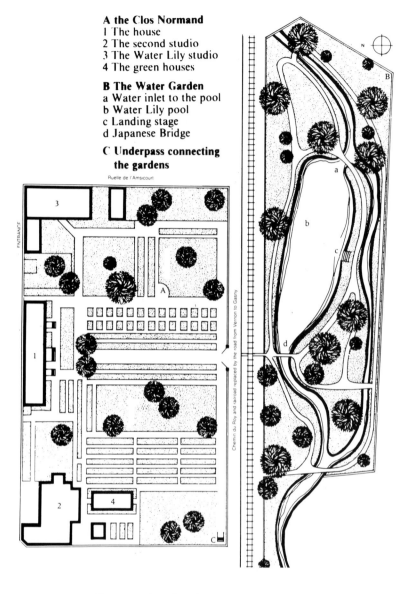

A the Clos Normand
1 The house
2 The second studio
3 The Water Lily studio
4 The green houses

B The Water Garden
a Water inlet to the pool
b Water Lily pool
c Landing stage
d Japanese Bridge

**C Underpass connecting
the gardens**

Shapes on the right of the plan are relatively conventional for Monet's day. His originality is seen in the lay-out of the Clos Normand (left), with its 'paint box' flower beds, reminiscent of vegetable gardens and Holland's tulip fields.

and reds, are significantly close to each other in the flower beds. The result is intensity, harmony and sometimes shock. The irreverent critic, Nancy Banks-Smith, reviewing a television programme on Giverny, spoke of Claude Monet as a man 'with a noisy taste in flowers'. She went on to describe

> Roses *with bright pink faces stand to attention and innumerable lilies blow their orange bugles. ... Purple and red tulips float like balloons on stalks. Purple geraniums and orange nasturtiums grow together. ... You must step back to focus the shimmering, stinging colours and, in fact, they make you step back.*

She was agreeing with the garden writer Stephen Lacey: 'Anyone stepping through the gate would be knocked for six by the colour. Especially anyone used to English gardens and the gentle drifts of harmonious colour. Monet really socks it to you.' An admirable summary of Giverny!

But no one who is interested in planting could visit Giverny without looking at the water-lily ponds. These are of the greatest beauty, when one of the two wisteria – first lilac and then white – is in flower on the Japanese bridge, and reflections of light off water and glinting lily leaves dematerialize the whole scene. The slender cascades of weeping willow leaves create a kind of rain of vertical marks that counterbalance the horizontal surfaces. This is visionary – and also typical of a period when water-lilies were high fashion. Gertrude Jekyll, for instance, devotes pages to them. Monet's difference was, once again, to take an idea so far, to the point where its realization alters our sensations. It is also of its time in that the costs of such an enterprise today would be astronomic. Moreover, were he living today, Monet would be most unlikely to overcome the objections he encountered in his own day and be allowed to alter the course of a tributary of the River Epte to water his lily garden.

auburn hair of a girl in Renoir's *Les Parapluies* (c1883) gives additional life to the blues that dominate the picture. So in all Monet's flowers there are such colour interactions.

But he does not stop there. Colours that are closely related to each other, like yellows, oranges, crimsons

Sheila Jackson in London

Monet painted a living picture on a scale almost unimaginable. Sheila Jackson uses a small canvas. Her garden is only 7.3m (24ft) wide and its depth tapers from 6 to 4.3m (20 to 14ft). But as Gertrude Jekyll remarked: 'The size of a garden has very little to do with its merit.' Sheila is, among other things, a book illustrator, and this is the clue to how she has developed her garden and channelled her plant collector's lust, so that neither in composition, nor in colour, has she attempted to crowd too much into the picture.

The garden lies, facing south, between a tall Victorian house in Camden Town and a main railway line. Sheila looks out on to it from her workroom win-

dows, and so her intention was, twenty-five years ago, to give herself an attractive view, and to clothe the fence that hides the railway, in winter as well as in summer. Today this vital backdrop includes an *Elaeagnus pungens* 'Maculata', a stand of bamboo, a *Mahonia japonica* and the evergreen *Clematis armandii* garlanding four chimney pots, each 2.1m (7ft) high, which were taken down from the roof several years ago. These add a touch of drama, which is appropriate, for Sheila has a life-long association with the theatre, and she designed the costumes for the popular television series, *Upstairs, Downstairs*. Her boundary with the adjacent back yard is a rich weave of ivy, rose ('Climbing Little White Pet') and *Clematis* x *jouiniana* 'Praecox'. So the scene is set for events in her garden.

The key to her garden is that she thinks in terms of the illustrations that she is so accustomed to laying out

Sheila Jackson's plan of her garden shows how carefully she has evolved shapes and heights.

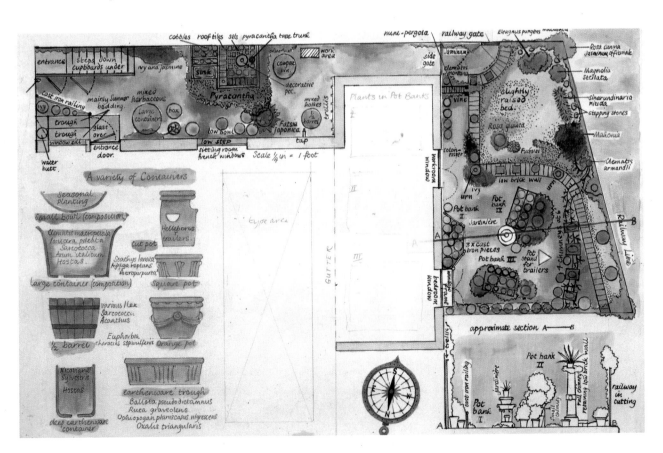

LEFT: Seen from the corner entrance, the backyard seems part of a larger garden because of the diagonal sight-line and plant-covered boundaries at the far side.
OPPOSITE: Colours are strictly limited in this minute backyard, but good foliage shapes, such as the euchomis on top of the plant stand and thoughtfully chosen performers, such as *Hebe salicifolia*, ensure visual interest.

Mahonia haematocarpa: these and many others bring in the tints of glaucous blue, grey-blue and all the other subtleties that garden writers struggle to express. Sheila's garden is, rather like the White Garden at Sissinghurst, a small and quite difficult lay-out given coherence by a restricted colour range.

Another of the constraints of the garden has helped to provide a theme and style. There is only one flower bed and it is small. Faced in the main by a concrete floor when she began her gardening, Sheila decided, first, to raise that bed and, second, to grow many of her plants in pots. If proof were needed that constraints can be fruitful, here it is. The plants like their pots, which are well-crocked and supplied with decent soil; the sharp drainage means that many come through damp London winters where, planted in gardens, they would likely die through water-logging of the roots. This method of growing them also means that Sheila has only to move the pots around to 'get things right by eye'.

As for her illustrated pages, each is different in character. From her window, you look out at one founded on *Hedera helix* ssp. *helix* 'Ivalace', which wraps around the flower bed's retaining wall. It is flanked by the fishbone-like branches of *Cotoneaster horizontalis*. Above, the composition rises into *Hosta fortunei* var. *aureomarginata* next to *H.* 'Halcyon' and above this, the pale pungency of alyssum, *Aurinia saxatilis* var. *citrina*. This teams with *Achillea* 'Moonshine'. Bowles's gold grass, *Milium effusum* 'Aureum', is surmounted by the cloud-like blooms of *Euphorbia stricta*, which create a gold haze in the afternoon sun.

on a page. The garden is, in a way, put together as a series of colour plates, an idea to which I will return. The underlying theme is that she realized early on that she would have to restrict her colour range, for the space is so small that too many colours would cause chaos. There are no blue flowers. But there is no lack of blue in the picture because it is provided by foliage. *Euphorbia characias* ssp. *wulfenii*, *Festuca glauca*, purple sage, *Corydalis wilsonii*, *Hosta* 'Halcyon',

Quite a different effect is produced by a group of which the prevailing colours are dark. Here there is *Heuchera micrantha* var. *diversifolia* 'Palace Purple', purple sage and, at the back, *Berberis thunbergii* 'Atropurpurea Nana'. The spear leaves of *Cordyline australis* provide accent. An uncompromising purple is given by *Oxalis triangularis*, and brilliant scarlet first by *Lychnis* x *arkwrightii* and later by *Lobelia* 'Queen Victoria'. Too much of the deep red shades would be oppressive; the gentle green of *Euphorbia mellifera* provides relief and a marvellous area of pattern, not to mention the honey-scent of its flowers in late spring. *Darmera peltata* (syn. *Peltiphyllum peltatum*) also provides pattern, on a much bigger scale. Because it is grown in a pot – placed within a washing up bowl, the arrangement masked by large pebbles – its large, round leaves sometimes end the year a brilliant deep reddish-brown. This dark group of plants brings depth and richness to the whole garden.

Sheila's favourite sheet of illustrations is provided by a bank of pots built up against the wall of the house. A decorative piece of Victorian wrought-iron work from a balcony leans against the base of the composition. It is left rusting because the colour is friendly to the plants. The position is the sunniest in the garden and the plants are variations on pale sulphur yellow, but not lacking a touch of sharpness, introduced by *Lonicera nitida* 'Baggesen's Gold'. This is toned down by *Coronilla valentina* 'Citrina', chalky pale in leaf. *Correa backhouseana* has dusky little green obovate leaves, but small, creamy, bell-shaped flowers. *Hamamelis mollis* adds a dashing touch of yellow in mid-winter, and its generous round leaves calm down the fussiness of small leaves in the summer. Around the base all sorts of inventive touches appear in summer: an unusual pale yellow nasturtium, for example, and the marvellous blue-green leaf of the horned poppy, *Glaucium corniculatum*, whose flowers depart from the yellow theme into orange. *Nicotiana glauca*, which seeds itself in walls in the south of France and grows

tough and shrub-like, in a pot in an urban back yard is quite demure, producing flowers that are truly the colour of egg yolks.

It is often the fate of gardens and gardeners to discover that Gertrude Jekyll has been before them. She noted ahead of Sheila Jackson how well different kinds of pale yellow harmonize. This colour plate does indeed repay a lot of looking, partly because the colour of the page, that is the house-wall, is just the right tint of faintest yellow. In addition, the planting here is vertical, because Sheila had to deal with the problem of a tall blank wall and a drain-pipe coming down it. There is a special pleasure in the way the plants take the eye upwards, particularly when you see how convenient *Akebia quinata* finds the old warrior of a drain-pipe, and how well the almost black flowers show off against the spiralling stems that go galloping up it.

These plates of illustrations would not do us much good if the minute garden didn't allow us to circulate, but it does. The path is narrow but positive. By its start to the side of the house, there is a small arch, which invites one to pause at the view thus framed before taking a few steps forwards and a turn around the Victorian pot stand that is the physical centre of the garden. The scope for movement gives the place extra vitality, for it allows many different points of view. The pleasure that these offer is something like that of turning a miniature sculpture around in the hand and enjoying the discovery of so many facets in so small a compass.

Visitors do not just take a few steps and a turn, because the plant interest is so intense and there are so many pleasing details in the way plants are juxtaposed. A tour of the garden can take a surprisingly long time – although not quite as long as a tour of Giverny. I have scarcely hinted at the beautiful plants, both common and rare to be found here, but her example shows how the selective eye of the artist can work along with the appetites of the plant collector to create a rare and beautiful backyard. The secret is visual discipline.

Derek Jarman at Dungeness

Derek Jarman acquired Prospect Cottage at Dungeness, on the coast of the English Channel, gale-torn yet with the highest number of hours of sun in the British Isles, in 1985. It was a dramatic change of habitat for a cosmopolitan film-maker based in London. His decision to spend long periods at Prospect Cottage followed his discovery that he was HIV positive. When he started to make a garden in 1985, he went right back into his childhood experience to create a place that against all the odds feels good and whole. He also brought to the garden all his experience as a writer, painter – for he had trained at the Slade School of Art in London – and theatre designer. This long 'cultivation of the eye' in someone who took an almost iconoclastic role in challenging society's conventions accounts for the quality of the visual decisions evident here. You are aware that an eye has been looking that doesn't just see plants growing.

This garden is wholly determined by its landscape, which is powerful, flat, bleached and partially degraded. It is open to all the elements. To the northeast lies the sea. To the south is Dungeness Power Station, like a giant rising from the horizon. Behind the little house are shallow pools, punctuated by gorse, brambles, tufts of grass and the occasional stunted elder. North is the fifteenth-century tower of Lydd church, known as 'the cathedral of the marsh' for its impact on the flatness. In this incredibly spare landscape the only luxuries are the light and, if you choose to look at your feet, the shingle beds that a hundred years ago were the sea shore. Inland, you have to make do with shingle extracted from river-beds or quarries. But this is the real thing, and all the richer in tones for its long voyage, rolled round in time as well as place, from the sea beds.

There is no hedge, no wall; this is quite a shock. But the boundaries are there, laid out in the shingle by sea-washed timbers, and punctuated by spiky poles from

Crambe maritima (sea kale), seen back left, is the plant genius of Prospect Cottage at Dungeness. The amazing garden scene, of plants and sculptural elements, does not attempt to evade what the twentieth century has done to the landscape.

piers that have capitulated to the sea. The garden is a place you enter for all that you open no gate. It runs some 40m (130ft) along in front of Prospect Cottage and then 27m (88ft) down the side and along the back till it meets the little extension: a wrap-around garden.

The plants are everywhere in dialogue with trophies from the sea that have taken on a life as sculpture, and I found I could hardly separate the two. You feel both equally came from the landscape. Jarman spotted hag-stones – stones with a hole in them – and turned them into a necklace on the ground. A broken eel spear stands like an echo of Neptune. Broken whelk shells decorate spiked timbers sticking up out of the shingle. Another worn piece of wood looks like an ox. Here is a fragment of a plough; there is a tripod of tangled metal rods that once were wartime fence posts. Taken singly, each would have the random suggestiveness of the *objet trouvé*, but together they work with the plants to produce a powerful symbolic effect, at once disturbing and, because there are so many mandala shapes on the ground, consoling. The dark tones of rusting metal show, like exclamation marks, against the paleness of floor and plants. They make the planting important.

The plants are survivors, like the flotsam and jetsam. Pared down unlike the way they look in suburban gardens, they gleam, constantly recording the wind. The key individual is sea kale, *Crambe maritima*, which Jarman originally gathered as seed from the sea shore. In midsummer the clouds of flowers had turned into ghostly white seed pods. The strong, vast, bluish leaves provide a shelter for sage, and their bold yet delicate shapes create a plant sculpture to counterpoint the wood and metal. The use of such native plants as this and sea pinks, *Armeria maritima*, gives 'coherence and a sense of place'.

On to this plant population, Jarman grafted other

Planting at Prospect Cottage is built up from the plants found locally.

In July the garden is afire with colour, but early and late in the year the shingle's rich tones and greys and greens of foliage are equally satisfying.

non-native plants that tolerated the site. The curry plant, *Helichrysum italicum*, santolinas and even large-leaved verbascums, *Verbascum* 'Vernale', which you might think would be vulnerable to the salty gales, flourish and, because they are so well suited to their habitat, provide foliage colour over a long period. Their greys, whites and bluish-greens complement the shingle and are shown off by the dark rusting metals.

Some protection is afforded by the cottage's back extension. Here there are softer plants, acanthus, cardoons, *Cynara cardunculus* and even a *Crambe cordifolia* which makes a rhyme, so to speak, with the *C. maritima*, which runs like a visual motif through the garden. Away from the shelter of the house, an elder bush, *Sambucus nigra*, ringed by a rusty chain is decisively pruned back to 46cm (18in). In the lea of the house, another is allowed to reach several feet.

In the spring and earlier summer there are brilliant colours: tulips, californian poppies, roses, mallows and kniphofias, for example. Even in late August, when the colours are necessarily quieter, the effects are satisfying. The weird lichen-white of *Mertensia maritima* ssp. *asiatica* interacts with the green of a piece of old copper. A cistus leaf looks rich in colour next to pallid santolinas and the even colder silver of *Artemisia* 'Powis Castle'. The black background presence of the cottage, with its bright intense yellow woodwork, grounds the more pallid greys and blues and silvers. Christopher Lloyd loved the place but wondered why anyone would bother with irises in an environment so unfriendly to their already fragile and ephemeral flowers.

While the majority of Jarman's plants are equipped naturally to survive the tough conditions, the irises and the roses, including *R. pimpinellifolia*, look healthy but are plainly embattled, and thereby add another note.

The spikes of their foliage add a vertical hatching that contrasts neatly with the wind-blown cushiony plants.

The last thing this garden displays is artfulness. At a casual glance, it melts into its surroundings. If you were to view it from the road, you might think that there were just some old bits and pieces stuck in the shingle. But there are overtones of magic. No attempt is made to grow plants up the great totem pole near the back of the house. This chunky piece of wood stands, drawing its vertical strength from the ground, in a great low collar of santolinas. The garden makes you wonder what is buried in the shingle. In another context it might have the resonance of some strange eastern cemetery. Here the plants, hugging the shingle, remind us that what is in the ground is life. The vast *Crambe cordifolia* especially is a reminder of the earth's power.

In a way the local landscape is cruel, and has been cruelly treated – witness the power station dumped on it. There is nothing of the favoured site that gardeners usually seek, such as that to be found at Denmans or even, relatively speaking, in Beth Chatto's garden. Although he had to spend months removing crops of rubbish that emerged from the shingle, Jarman did not view the local environment negatively. Like Steve Martino in the different environment of the Sonoran Desert of Arizona, he worked in a creative collaboration with it by choosing plants, local and otherwise, that found, with the gardener's care, a nourishing environment. The obvious parallel is that Jarman turned his own ravaged internal landscape, with the HIV positive result that led to his death in 1994, into an amazing garden. It is an artist's because of the considered and original decisions that are evident, together with a sense of the enormous fun – as well as the work – involved in its making. It is also evidence of the artist's capacity if need be to make something out of personal suffering that addresses the private dilemma and at the same time has the power to communicate with people; in this sense it might be compared with Van Gogh's sunflowers and irises.

Derek Jarman wrote the following poem about his garden.

I waited a lifetime to build my garden,
I built my garden with the colours of healing,
On the sepia shingle at Dungeness.
I planted a rose and then an elder,
Lavender, sage, and *Crambe maritima*,
Lovage, parsley, santolina,
Hore hound, fennel, mint and rue.
Here was a garden to soothe the mind,
A garden of circles and wooden henges,
Circles of stone, and sea defences.
And then I added the rust brown scrap,
A float, a malin and old tank trap.
Dig in your soul with the compost from Lydd,
Cuttings, divisions are placed in frames,
Protected from rabbits with neat wood cones.
My garden sings with the winds in winter.
Braving the salt which sails in plumes,
From the rolling breakers that gnaw the shingle.
No Hortus Conclusus, my seaside garden.
With poet's sleeping and dreaming of daisies.
I'm wide awake on this Sunday morning.
All the colours are present in this new garden.
Purple iris, imperial sceptre;
Green of the buds breaking on elder;
Browns of the humus, and ochre grasses;
Yellows in August on *Helichrysum*,
That turns in September to orange and brown;
Blue of the bugloss, and self-sown cornflower;
Blue of the sage and winter hyacinth;
Pink and white roses blowing in June;
And the scarlet rosehips, fiery in winter;
The bitter sloes to make sweet gin.
Brambles in autumn,
And gorse in the spring.

Touches of Wildness

Joyce Robinson and John Brookes at Denmans, Gilles Clément at Parc André-Citroën, Paris, The Jacobs at Montrose, Victoria

There is wild and there is wild. For someone who wants to make a butterfly habitat or a beetle bank, wild means nettles, buddleias and stacks of rotting wood. In such a garden interest in the planting is likely to take second place to the aims of creating habitats and attracting wild life. But for the urban gardener, the character of the wild that most conveniently translates to a private garden arises from the contrast of plants – soft, textural, ephemeral – with some natural hard material. What I would ideally like to have around my garden is a Welsh

Groups of poppies, wild brassicas and grasses such as these seen growing in Turkey can provide inspiration for more considered planting schemes.

dry-stone wall, with pennywort, ferns and herb Robert, stained burgundy by its dry position, set against the greys of stone flecked with lichens. An impossible habitat in a London garden, unfortunately; but the message of hard against soft, distinct edge against blurred edge, a low-key range of colours and the character of certain communities of plants, can be translated into garden terms. When one thinks of ways in which the idea of the wild might lead to a distinct planting style, several possibilities arise. One is where plants seen in the wild have provided the original inspiration, which the gardener then transforms into a more gardenesque style that, through plant choice and horticultural method, retains a link with the original vision. Such is my first example.

Joyce Robinson and John Brookes at Denmans

Denmans lies near Chichester in Sussex. Behind and to the north is a magnificent tract of countryside, running up to the Sussex downs. The vision of plants in the wild that inspires this garden comes straight from a holiday in Greece. Joyce Robinson had for some years gardened with her husband at Denmans when, on holiday one spring in the 1970s, she saw the stony Greek island of Delos in flower. Already a little bored with the medium of grass and paving, she realized that she could imitate the flora she had seen by planting into shingle. What she discovered was that the good drainage this gives to plants is more important than the rich feeding that accompanies the traditional border.

The old enclosed garden is central to Denmans, but the garden overall is characterized by the flowing lines and balance to be found in abstract art.

For a start, she says, find the local gravel that harmonizes with your site and its walls, and if possible let it be water-washed, not crushed stone. In the southeast of England, for example, sandy coloured shingle is easily available, while in other areas it might be grey or pink.

At Denmans this technique shows up most distinctly where a dried up river bed has been created across a gentle south-facing slope. The underlying idea is to create a planting environment and then grow in it those plants for which it might be a natural habitat. After that, allow some self-seeding to take place. Thus, in one part of this river bed a spiky thistle collected in Portugal drifts around, over the shingle and up against large stones that are part of the river bed effect. Behind some of the stones is a simple mound of *Fatshedera lizei*. What emerges is slightly abstract and spare, but rich in textures and warm in colouring.

It is the result of collaborative gardening between Joyce Robinson and John Brookes who some years ago

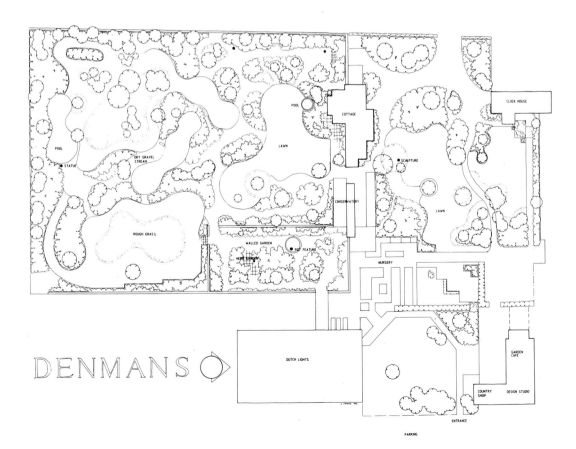

DENMANS

Lines of grass and shingle work with planting – especially
a riot of verbascums – to lead the eye onwards.

took over the running of the gardens. He has carried
on her principles while inevitably grafting on to it his
own way of planting. Sometimes this involves choosing
a hybrid where Mrs Robinson might perhaps have chosen a species. 'He will keep on putting in more exotic
plants,' she says, waving towards a nearby *Hydrangea
arborescens* 'Annabelle', 'and then it begins to look
like a herbaceous border.' This combination of naturalism and exoticism is perfectly harmonious. The
Mediterranean note, which is a reminder of holidays,
is enriched by the judicious choice of garden hybrids,
and there is an enjoyable tension between planting that
is at one moment quite spare, only to sweep off the

next into lusher effects. But Joyce Robinson's planting
style also blends with John Brookes' acute eye for the
formal qualities of plants. This connects closely with
the character of his garden design, which has always
drawn on abstract art.

The result is that there are signs of a casual, natural look and profusion, but they are tempered. While
self-seeding is evident everywhere, at the same time
there is both visual control and gardening skill. Those
seedlings are kept that place themselves tellingly, as
when a grey-leaved *Verbascum bombyciferum* appears
at the foot of a cotoneaster. Even when the planting
looks most natural, selection has been at work, dis-
pelling visual muddle and creating rhythms and
patterns among the plants.

What is most unwild are the bold, clear edges of the

grassed areas, a green sea pushing against a shore of pebbles. The richness of this old-fashioned sward against the astringency of the shingle is a huge asset. Contrast seems to be all-important, whatever the style of the gardening. But the pastures have their own geometry, as the broad green ribbons of mown grass wrap around more meadowy islands, full of bulbs and cut once a year in July. Balances of this kind add to the sense of well-being.

Planting is used to help to create views that draw the visitor on. Seen from a distance, the curves of shingle and grass work with a canopy of prunus and, at ground level, bergenia to create a visual frame. The

Euphorbia characias is used across the site to provide structure as well as its animated light green flowers in spring and early summer.

shapes and planes go together. They are the product of a trained eye that looks, and makes decisions about where to prune, where to leave well alone and where to intervene and clear away.

I have started out in the open at Denmans. But to reach this area the visitor first passes through the walled garden. The views and the experience of this space, like those of formal yew topiary, are to do with solid geometry. There are abstract shape and well-moulded form, but loosened by the freedom of abstract art. Euphorbias and well-clipped box are repeated through the area. *Phormium tenax* provides large-scale spikes. Translated into sculpture, one might say the box is Henry Moore, and the phormium is bundles of tall, thin Giacometti people.

Within the garden the soft foliage of a *Robinia pseudoacacia* 'Frisia' provides a green-gold canopy,

Self-seeding sisyrinchium and verbascums at Denmans are a reminder of plants growing in the wild.

forming a contrast with the adjacent flint and brick walls. Although enclosed, the garden is linked to the landscape beyond. Towards the northern wall stems lead the eye up, through kniphofias and the amazing milky grey-green of *Berberis temolaica*. They encounter the soft green leaves of a catalpa before boughs of ash in a distant hedgerow drift off skywards.

The planting at Denmans is in one sense svelte

because form is so important and because key plants, like variegated box, are trimmed. Trees and shrubs are chosen for their strong leaves, as with *Aesculus pavia*, or their structural qualities, such as *Acer capillipes*. To draw attention to the original inspiration offered by the Greek spring flowers may seem to be overemphasizing the note of the wild, but apart from the particularly well-groomed areas around the house, the planting has an easy, natural look. This is partly because of the self-seeders, like verbascums and euphorbias and the tall *Verbena bonariensis*, that are in evidence across the garden. But it is also to do with the shingle medium, and the way that it simply disappears among the plants, without any formal division between path and planting area. It comes too from the planting, which evokes the Mediterranean, where nature is more kempt than in the lusher landscape of northern Europe.

The basic colour range is of buffs and yellows, starting with the shingle and leading up to the clear yellow of verbascum and the exotic brilliance of the yellow robinia. Balancing these there are masses of colours, like the metallic blues of eryngiums and the purples of sages, that hint at colour complementaries. There are lots of the soft grey-green of cistus leaves – another reminder of the Mediterranean *maquis*. Brighter colours are more occasional highlights. Such planting both revels in the soft brilliant light – the sea is only a few miles away – and suggests the sun.

What the Robinson-Brookes collaboration has done at Denmans is to select from plants and landscapes in the wild to make a garden vocabulary revolving around form, volume, verticals and horizontals, suggesting an orderliness in nature – as indeed there is in natural vegetation in the south of France. But this is only one version of the wild. There are others that are less oriented to hot, sunny, dry climates and memories of summer holidays.

Gilles Clément at Parc André-Citroën, Paris

Quite a different piece of invention is to be found in this new and exciting park, in the shape of Gilles Clément's Garden of Movement. The whole park, which is extremely popular, provides all manner of displays, such as a black garden, a series of conservatories, fountains and waterways. But one of its interests is that it is pulsing with ideas that underpin the outward show. The Garden of Movement is discovered at the end of a series of gardens on the theme of colour, in which built elements, such as the water channels that divide them, play a large and effective part. Indeed, most of this park is formally laid out, deliberately echoing other formal parks along the left bank of the Seine; so Clément's cultivated wilderness comes as a complete shock.

When they first see this garden, some people ask if any gardening goes on at all. Others see a mixture of

Massed fennel abuts a group of *Rosa glauca* in the Garden of Movement. Large blocks of one kind of plant create form and pattern.

exuberance and cultivation, a kind of reassuring wild place where there is an underlying order while the plants are allowed a great deal of freedom. Clément has often waged war on the 'lawn' during his career, and here he has replaced it by a meadow. Walking across this takes you through pockets and dingles, full of *Salvia sclarea* var. *turkestanica* and verbascums growing in grass that is thick with vetch and clover. The meadow plants reach the shoulders of a child.

Beyond the meadowy effects the planting builds in height, through tree lupins and saponaria (wild soapwort) towards banks of shrubs, which on a sunny summer day provide a sense of protection at one's back. Here are dog roses but also, bringing in a note of the exotic, *Rosa moyesii*, with its long sprays of little, single flowers. The natural shades off, too, into stands of *R. glauca*. Growing into these is fennel with its profuse soft clouds billowing in the wind. *R. glauca*'s grey-pink foliage and the fennel's gentle green are excellent foils for each other, and the planting – and self-seeding – is on such a scale that it generates a strong colour experience.

Genuine wild meadows and hedgerows will tend to offer little ripples of colour and endless small

Tree lupins suggest wild origins at the same time as being shapely. White saponaria adds incisiveness to the scheme.

variations on many-flowers-on-a-stem, an apparently pleasing fuss until you look closely at the detail. The generous plantings of the Garden of Movement mean that the groups acquire form and mass. These have a tranquil effect, like the calming large leaves of the verbascum, foxglove and symphytum (comfrey) in the grass. The wild and the exotic intertwine: a homely sclary grows up through the branches of a *Parrotia persica*, whose branches at all times of year have a pleasing rhythm. Such occasional exotic subjects give structure to the planting.

This garden lacks formal boundaries, unlike the theme gardens preceding it. But towards one end, masses of *Arundinaria nitida* half-close off the view, the tightly packed bamboo stems making a sort of visual full stop. No foliage talks so much and so evocatively to itself in the wind. It is also a singularly appropriate choice for a Garden of Movement.

The lack of *haute coiffure* has aroused mixed reactions; but the place is user-friendly. In summer children play and explore, and people picnic around the low banqueting tables, furnishings that complement the planting but do not obscure the view, and pleasantly evoke a *déjeuner sur l'herbe*. Perhaps French painting's rich tradition of crowds of people enjoying themselves, whether in festivals in the Tuileries gardens, on the *grande Jatte* or under umbrellas in the rain, predisposes Parisians to make the most of Sunday in this magnificent new park.

Clément's philosophy is intriguing. In his own garden in Normandy he abandoned the tyranny of lawns and over a number of years observed the performance and development of plant communities in a piece of fallow ground. From what he learnt he was able to work out the sort of garden he wanted. He is fascinated by the change and flux in the plant landscape, and the energies that enable plants to reclaim a piece of abandoned ground. In the impenetrable zones of brambly undergrowth and mud in the wild he sees a power like that of the unconscious. His gardens of movement, with their areas of dense vegetation barring our way, aim to give this power back to gardening.

Most of all this garden in Parc André-Citroën embodies movement. The plants move in the wind – fennel is a sensitive recorder here – and through the seasons. In addition, there will be movement over the years, for visitors will never see quite the same garden in successive years. This is quite a profound shift from convention; Sissinghurst, for example, has not essentially changed since I first saw it in 1968. Courage is needed to try out Clément's ideas, but there is no real reason why we should expect permanence in the appearance of our gardens, a permanence that isolates them from the shifting, developing plant communities evolving in the wild. Clément's wild is not woolly; it has great aesthetic appeal and is immensely evocative.

The Jacobs at Montrose, Victoria

'Sissinghurst', reads a caption to a photograph of the tower seen across the orchard, 'is essentially a country garden, with formal enclosures melting easily into the wild.' What sort of wild is the ultra-domesticated Kentish countryside, that teems with signs of a long history of English culture? 'Wild' is decidedly relative. When gardens are put into an Australian setting, 'wild' starts to mean something different, a landscape that was alien to settlers precisely because it was not a Kentish sort of wild.

An Australian 'wild' garden means one that uses native plants. Rodger and Gwen Elliot are leading experts in these and the species that can be used in

Eucalypts are a great glory of the Australian landscape. Here, stems of *Eucalyptus leucoxylon* ssp. *megalocarpa* bring definition into the clumps of small-leaved plants and, together with the gently curving path, take the eye towards the mountains in the distance.

cultivation. What they took on was a site of some 2 hectares (5 acres) on which the contractor had left only eucalypts and some pines (*Pinus radiata*), which were removed because they were not indigenous. Within ten years the lower planting had reappeared, largely the result of a policy of simply removing seedlings that were not wanted. The place had the appearance of regenerated bushland, in which eucalypts and grasses in particular linked it with the larger landscape.

The inflections of such a garden are different from anything to be found in the West. Its essence is that it follows the natural contours of the land, and it is bound together and given form by, above all, the eucalypts, with their beautiful trunks and bark and their noble structure. They provide something for the eye to rest on, for most Australian native shrubs – such as grevilleas and leptospermums – have small, indeterminate leaves that are neither glossy nor matt, and can consequently present an amorphous appearance. Of themselves they cannot bring form to the garden, although some woody

OPPOSITE: *Dampiera linearis* illustrates the glowing blues found in Australian flora. *Jacksonia scoparia's* grey stems are a foil for *Boronia muelleri* 'Sweet Serenade'.

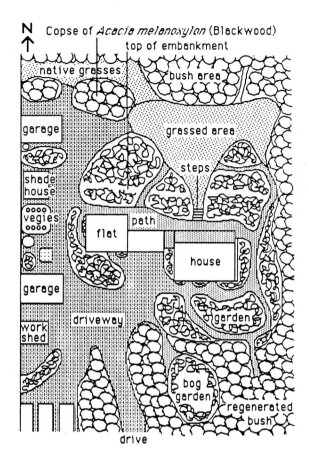

shrubs make a good gesture, such as upright bottle brushes and banksias, that are used in this garden as sentry features. A European or American eye can look at the endless small leaves and be rather baffled – as doubtless Australian gardeners once were. Hence the importance of the tall trees, the eucalypts and blackwoods, in leading the eye – in this case towards Victoria's Dandenong Ranges in the background.

This garden has been enriched by the planting of thousands of Australian native plants. So new is the field that little or nothing is known of how some of these will behave in cultivation. Other native plants, from many parts of Australia, increase the interest. Nonetheless, the garden looks like an intensification of the natural landscape rather than anything separated from it. And this was the Elliots' intention: to create something that merged into what lay around it. Fine gravel paths seem to wander away indistinctly, yet are significant events. Ellis Stones, the aptly-named Australian garden designer who had a genius for working with boulders and creating natural-looking outcrops of rock, wrote of the way a wandering track might give special interest to the landscape, and so it is with these paths. The whole character is not that of spectacle, but something quieter and ultimately more profound – like the landscape itself.

The colours are typically soft, grey-greens and other muted versions of green. Only around the house do they brighten, just as more flower colour is concentrated in the ornamental garden (where there are also Californian plants that are suited to the Australian conditions). Around the front door native plants – dendrobium, phebalium, eriostemon – are grown in pots, which can provide the form and structure that is absent from the plants themselves. Australia possesses a number of brilliant blue flowers and these – in particular *Dampiera linearis* – provide colour over many months.

Regenerated bush – including eucalypts, wattles (acacias) and grasses – screens the house from the east, while the area around the house is gardened to provide changing 'living pictures' throughout the year.

A great glamour of Australia are the birds, brilliant and vocal, with their extraordinary musical cadences. The garden now supports more than fifty kinds. The Elliots have selected from and added to what can be found in the Australian landscape to make a visually satisfying garden that forms part of the food chain precisely because it is married to the natural world around it. To achieve this a major readjustment has taken place in Australia in the perception of what constitutes a garden. This in itself is a creative act.

Now the Elliots have moved on to make another garden and Elspeth and Garry Jacobs look after Montrose.

Gardens and Ecology

Beth Chatto's Gravel Garden, Rosemarie Weisse, Munich Westpark, Wolfgang Oehme and James van Sweden, the Offutt Garden

Today gardens and ecology are often mentioned in the same breath, but something of a paradox is involved. A garden can never be an ecosystem, that subtle dynamic of relationships between environment and organisms, if only because it is never going to be self-sustaining. The idea of a garden spells out human interference, from soil structure and pH to irrigation. Because, too, we want gardens to give us pleasure and because many of us think of them in aesthetic terms, we often try to override natural time-scales, which in the wild bring about constant change in the plant communities. Whereas an acre left to itself in a temperate country would eventually end up as woodland, the gardener usually tries to prevent a jungly state.

The familiar beauty of Sissinghurst depends on time arrested, not just because the Nicolsons' gardening ideas have been carried on more or less intact, but also because – as in most well-loved and beautiful gardens – the vegetation is prevented from acting out growth, warfare and death, as it would if left to itself. A tourist crossing the Alps at the end of the eighteenth century peered into the Alpine forests and came up with the insight of 'woods decaying, never to be decayed' – rather a good description of one sort of ecosystem, but a dreary prospect for the human soul that wants to be surrounded with the scenes of hope and constant renewal that a garden can provide.

If there are few places on the face of the earth where there has ever been a natural garden paradise, there are at least inspiring and beautiful examples of gardens that incorporate genuinely ecological principles. Of my three examples, one is in Britain, one in Germany and one in the United States, and each uses the ecological idea in rather different ways, showing how it can be adapted to express a personal style.

Taller grasses and spires of kniphofias emerge from layers of sedums, while stachys provides a carpet. The planting structure here is very firm.

Beth Chatto's Gravel Garden

In Britain Beth Chatto has been creating her gardens and plant nursery near Colchester since 1960. Originating as the unfarmable part of her husband's fruit orchards, the three main garden areas offer every sort of gardening: hot and dry on the poor sand and gravel, shade and woodland where the soil is kinder, and a water garden in the low-lying, spring-fed hollow. She has used plants to suit each sort of environment in a part of East Anglia where, because the average rainfall does not exceed 50cm (20in) a year, drought or near-drought has been the main constant of her gardening life.

Just as constant has been the lifelong interest of Andrew Chatto in the natural habitat of garden flora, and he has provided the intellectual inspiration for her work. Her innovative gardens are based on ecologically sound principles: she finds plants that are happy with the given conditions and with each other, so that green communities are created in which each plant finds a niche to suit it.

Another influence was the sight of plants growing and flowering in natural associations in the Swiss Alps and the Mediterranean. An alpine flora can be hard to please in Britain, but the Chattos realized how relevant the Mediterranean vegetation of *maquis* and *garrigue* was to their East Anglian conditions: cistus, lavenders, euphorbias and bulbs grow in impoverished soils, with excellent drainage, contentedly at ease with one another.

Beth Chatto would also say there is a third sort of inspiration that comes from working with the soil, a partnership of hand and eye. As for the eye, there has been yet a fourth inspiration in her gardening. From the early 1950s until his death in 1981, the Chattos were friendly with Sir Cedric Morris. The East Anglian painter created a series of fabled gardens, the last of which was at Benton End, west of Colchester. Here plants rubbed shoulders with the students who came to

the art school that he ran jointly with his friend Lett Haines. Mrs Chatto's artistic eye shows in everything she touches, but where plants are concerned her eyes were opened by the possibilities revealed at Benton End. There were the plants Morris bred, especially the irises, and there were the plants he collected on his travels, often in Mediterranean parts. All these flourished on the sunny dry slopes of his garden: 'a bewildering, mind-stretching, eye-widening canvas of colour, textures and shapes, created primarily with bulbous and herbaceous plants.' There were, too, the plants he discovered locally, in hedgerows and the like, so that his garden was knit to the local landscape and its flora in all manner of ways. His portraits of human beings have been described as screaming likenesses; his numerous plant portraits are more benign but equally acute. Moreover, his pictures of groups of irises, cabbages and peppers, gathered together into still lifes, lucidly expound the way they occupy space. These visual lessons at Benton End must have been absorbed by Mrs Chatto, and I later include an account of how one particular painting helps in her planting.

A detail of Beth Chatto's gravel garden.

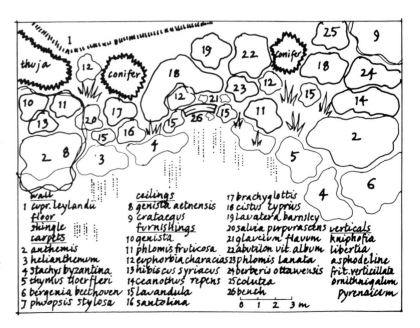

Alone, these brilliant flowers would be relatively ineffective.
A quiet and deep plant landscape, including grasses and
artemisias, makes them glow.

Of all her gardens, the gravel garden, started in
1991, is the most radical, and most spectacular. It is
radical because it is never, absolutely never, watered.
Plants that can thrive, even if with difficulty (for example, *Cestrum parqui* grows to half the size it manages
in conventional gardens), are admitted; those that cannot, such as hibiscus, which cannot cope with so little
moisture, are simply excluded. The policy points the
way to gardening in the not so distant future, when
water consumption, even in Britain, will outrun sup-
plies, and the garden hose will not be used. Although
quite unlike the traditional herbaceous border, for all
that she has read and admired Jekyll's books, the gravel garden is the most evocative of all her gardens. It is
not lush. There is an element of spareness about it, yet
it truly looks like the jewel box that Mrs Chatto's
gardening staff have called it.

Her initial idea for it came from dried-up river beds
seen in North America. What used to be her large
public car park is now a wide river of shingle (water-
washed pebbles). It continually breaks up into
tributaries where it encounters islands of planting. This
material is local, which is ideal for building a garden;
it is a light, sandy colour and glows, in winter as in
summer. It is an immensely sympathetic floor. Even
before Mrs Chatto has started to lead the eye among
the plants, the gravel 'river' flows wonderfully. It is
quite deliberately the main tune in the composition. It
also creates a permanent vista through a farm gate and
on to the fields and village houses beyond, giving a
strong feeling that this garden belongs in the larger
landscape.

There were established verticals from car park days.
A tall, deliciously textured, clipped hedge of
Cupressocyparis leylandii forms a geometric boundary
along one side. Reinforcing the verticals, a *Sorbus*

hupehensis var. *obtusa* interposes itself between the new garden planting and the hedge. Elsewhere Mrs Chatto has added a *Genista aetnensis* providing further height. These verticals are like foothills in front of a distant wall of mountains. Aesthetically, the hedge and trees are just right, but they are thirsty. As the plants are selected to cope with drought, this is not disastrous. The evergreen cupressus has a further virtue. It provides a great sense of protection as well as actively shielding the plants from the frequent fierce east winds. It is just as much 'great planting' as the rarities in the new garden.

In front of it, the planting comes forwards by some 11m (36ft), but not in a solid bank, nor uniformly graded in height from front to back. A comfortably wide path runs along by the hedge, so that clipping can be carried out, while the views into the planting from the main path present an image like that of the maquis, with little paths running through it. For the first metre or so by the path, the planting is loose. Here there might be bidens (cosmos), then a gap before a patch of *Kniphofia* 'Little Maid', another interval, and grouped *Centaurea pulcherrima*. A little further from them a group of *C. p.* 'Pulchra Major' links through. Further back the planting becomes rather denser, but still the paths taken by imaginary sheep thread their way through. Ashen-leaved phlomis, attendant *Salvia officinalis* var. *latifolia* 'Minor' and several *Euphorbia characias* casually form one group, and a foot away starts another grouping of a low broom and *Sedum* 'Herbstfreude' ('Autumn Joy'). Interpreting this through the eye of a painter, the space between forms, the 'negative' space, is as important as the forms themselves. Mrs Chatto thinks in terms of interlocking triangles, so that a euphorbia, say, may end one group and also start another. She achieves her ideals by placing plants, still in their pots, in grouped arrangements to study the effect before anything is planted. Once the plants are established, the effect depends on tending them and keeping an eye on their growth and spread in relation to each other. This sensitive 'hands on' care is a large part of Mrs Chatto's success.

If the plant heights went from low at the front to high at the back, this would be more like herbaceous border planting. Instead they undulate so that the vegetation can be curiously evocative of landform. In addition, tall stems growing near the path, such as *Verbena bonariensis*, fennel or one of any number of grasses, provide delectable screens, partly disclosing and partly hiding what lies behind them. As Mrs Chatto observes, there is a special pleasure in seeing plants against a void, rather than against a solid background.

Shapes for Mrs Chatto are the prime consideration in a garden, and, along with shapes, structure. For this reason the gravel garden is pleasing in winter as well as in summer. Here tall stems are retained, even if, as with the cardoon, the decrepit leaves must be snipped off. Her advice is: do not hasten to clear away in the autumn. Leave anything that has an interesting structure. Thinking in terms of verticals and cushion plants, she recognizes the pleasure of seeing plants profiled against the sky. Leaf shape is all-important, and numerous clumps and carpets of large leaves, like those of bergenia, verbascum and brunnera allow the eye respite from the fussiness of small leaves. In the *maquis*, a large stone or a rock may have the same effect, providing an interlude from the textured detail of cistus and lavender foliage.

The colour palette is also exceptionally satisfying. In summer it is spectacular, with spires of yellow verbascum and kniphofias, the brilliant magenta of *Gladiolus communis* ssp. *byzantinus*, and red or pink poppies plus a host of other pinks, purples and oranges. The glow of the gravel knits them together, and the dark hedge is a sober ever-present background. Sustaining the highlights is the sumptuous yet subdued palette provided by foliage. There are bergenias, metre upon metre of them, richly green in the summer and in many cases bronzed and wine-coloured in winter. Then

Parchment-coloured grasses and *Verbena bonariensis* enhance the garden into late autumn.

there are all the greys and blue-greens of sun-loving Mediterranean flora. Whereas in urban Britain one has to settle for *Brachyglottis* (syn. *Senecio*) 'Sunshine' to provide a warm whitish-grey, in her gravel garden, with its first-class drainage and high light levels, Mrs Chatto can grow great mounds of its more delicate relative, *Brachyglottis compacta*. Like Gertrude Jekyll, she believes that green is a colour, and you can find many sorts of green in this garden in February, tinged with blue, brown, grey or white. Much variety and richness within these greens comes from the grasses,

which bleach to parchment shades in winter. But for all the summer varieties of green, it is perhaps the range of yellows here that lift one out of a British 'green' experience and make the garden emotionally more charged.

This garden was created without drawn plans. The shapes of the planting areas and drifting paths were determined in the time-honoured manner by using a hosepipe laid on the ground. The soil was then extremely carefully prepared. A sub-soiler pulled behind the tractor was used to break up the compacted sub-soil, and plenty of humus was spread over the surface of almost pure sand and gravel. A purist 'wild' or 'ecological' gardener would not have pampered the plants in this way, and probably many would not have

Large blocks of the simple and familiar – such as the foreground anthemis – are vital throughout the garden.

survived, but Beth Chatto is a gardener and wanted to give hers a good start. She then grouped plants, working out where she wanted mass, 'the blocky things', what was needed in the middle ground and where she wanted all the verticals. When you put things on paper, she observes, they can become static, and some of the lovely flow and animation of this garden doubtless comes from the manner in which its structure was thought out on site rather than at the drawing board.

But what skill to visualize a landscape! This is where a painting comes into the story. In Mrs Chatto's words:

I have a view of rooftops in Portugal, painted by my old friend, the late Sir Cedric Morris. For years I admired it and was eventually able to buy Cedric's interpretation of warm tiled roofs, whitewashed walls and a bell tower carrying the eye up to the sky. But not before Cedric had warned me, 'Do not keep it if you are not happy with it. If it is not right in your house you will grow to hate it.' The picture belonged straight away, and gradually, as my garden has grown, I can see how much the strong architectural design of this painting has influenced my planting. The interlocking angles of roofscapes are repeated in the way I use plants and shrubs, making comfortable groups of different shapes and textures, with spaces between for the birds to fly through as the mind's eye drifts between the tall buildings in the picture to the hills beyond; while tall narrow trees, like the swamp cypress and the Dawn Redwood have become, for me, the church spires in my village.

Another metaphor that interprets her designing with plants is music. With the 'dried-up river bed' as a main tune, a line of melody turned into a visual shape as it were, she develops her motifs, allowing them to echo each another. There are constant repeats of euphorbia and sea poppy and of the verticals and soft billowing clouds of grasses in flower. All these create harmonies or, to change the metaphor yet again, the rhymes and rhythms of poetry. There is a sort of mobility in her thinking that transmits itself to the garden, and this mobility is especially evident in the gravel garden. It is to do with airy stems catching any passing breeze, and with the views that constantly evolve as one walks around and between the plants. One is a figure in a landscape, not merely a spectator looking at a picturesque herbaceous border. While the latter is an equally valid option, the former offers a deeper spatial experience.

Perhaps that is one reason why this gravel garden is such a stirring experience. Its sunny floor, its scents and sights, evoke holidays in the Mediterranean. But this has not happened by chance. The whole scheme grows out of repeated phrases and tone colours. Although it is a sensuous experience, much thought has gone into it, as would be the case with a piece of music or a painting. Beneath the sensory delights is a wonderful sense of structure, finding expression in the most evanescent of materials.

The gravel garden makes an interesting comparison with Denmans. Both share a Mediterranean inspiration of plants growing in scree or in the impoverished soil of the *maquis*. Hence the plant palettes overlap, and the horticultural methods are similar. One important difference is the site. Denmans is exceptionally favoured and inevitably, therefore, creates a lusher effect. Another is the personal style of the gardeners, the plant groups for which they have an especial liking and the ways in which they group plants and build them up. A third is that Denmans is a garden consciously designed around the sort of shapes to be found in abstract art. It has a different kind of self-consciousness from that of the Essex garden, where a natural example, the dried-up river bed of North America, is the starting point for its lay-out.

Mrs Chatto has long been a leader in planting styles in Britain and America. How does her latest experiment relate to what can be done in small gardens and urban conditions? Her gravel garden depends on strong light and excellent drainage, so that although winter may be wet and freezing, the plants' roots are protected by the gravelly medium. This also prevents water-logging and provides an insulating layer. Anyone setting out to make a garden in town is likely to encounter a good deal of shade, from trees or buildings or both, as well as soil full of builder's rubble and prone to the attentions of cats. The constant shade is an opportunity rather than a problem. Even a part of Mrs Chatto's gravel garden is somewhat overcast by a large oak tree, but the plants she has chosen for it flourish happily. Traditionally, improving the soil in town gardens has meant digging out the rubbish and enriching what is left, and this is nearly always necessary. Gardening writer Robin Lane-Fox recounts how he had wished to name one of his books 'Better Drains' but was prevented from doing so by his wife. But if we want to emulate Beth Chatto's latest adventure in planting, 'better drainage' had better be our motto. Our next garden will take this theme further.

Rosemarie Weisse, Munich Westpark

Beth Chatto's garden offers fresh and surprising ways of thinking. New ideas being carried out in Germany are likely to prove even more of a shock to conventional gardening wisdom: 'Impoverish the soil' and exercise 'calculated neglect.' What are the gardens in which such principles are practised?

One answer is Westpark in Munich, which arose as part of the 1983 Munich Garden Festival from a reclaimed industrial site – seemingly unpromising material for a garden. What actually greet the visitor to Westpark are large areas of flowers – some at the edge of woodland, some meadowy, some flowing across a rocky steppe. Irises, violas, potentillas, asphedoline and geraniums drift around each other. Sometimes they are blended with grasses, which in one place extend up a

hillside. Month after month the flowers come: lilies, lavender, kniphofias, delphiniums and day-lilies. Autumn brings asters and sedums, *Gaura lindheimeri*'s pink flowers continuing to float among them. *Pennisetum orientale* (fountain grass) and other grass seedheads extend the spectacle.

This amazing garden was developed by Rosemarie Weisse from the hemerocallis display commissioned from her for the Garden Festival. It is a revolution, challenging the monopoly of the herbaceous or perennial border, for it is low-maintenance, aesthetically delightful and based on ecological principles.

Instead of bringing together the most beautiful associations of border perennials and then having to fight

Carefully chosen plant communities create a long season of ever-changing colour. Little maintenance is required, but it must be skilled.

The planting philosophy here – large swathes of delphiniums and rudbeckias related to natural species – is akin to that of Oehme and van Sweden (see page 91).

against the odds to preserve them, the gardener works on the basis of what is happening in the natural landscape among the 'wild' perennials. Rosemarie Weisse and other like-minded gardeners in Germany use, for example, versions of delphiniums that occur in the wild or that are close to those found growing in the wild. Instead of planting them in one clump or one drift, she treats them as they might be found in the wild, with, say, one main clump in an area and smaller groupings drifting away as though they had self-seeded. These loose plantings are interwoven with other species, which themselves move out as if from parent groups. The effect, therefore, while looking natural, with the delightful random weaving to be found on a flowery hillside, has, in fact, been carefully designed.

The garden is based on wild perennials, but because this is an amenity garden in the city, from which people want the pleasure of a flowering season that is as long as possible and the excitement of an enriched form of gardening, these are joined by cultivars. Again, these are chosen because they are sociable and will not either rampage out of control or languish and disappear.

If the ground were prepared like that of a conventional border, such a garden could not occur. In a traditional border the soil offers conditions that are remote from those found in the wild, and it has traditionally had the role of producing extra-large flowers, blooms that will win prizes at horticultural shows. At Westpark the secret is, yet again, drainage, added to impoverishment and ecological understanding.

Because Westpark was created from an industrial gravel pit where there was no existing soil, preparations had to start from scratch. First the ground was contoured. Then a soil medium was laid to a depth of 40cm (16in) over the whole area, but the medium contained 20 per cent gravel, and a rather smaller percentage of peat and good top-soil. In the 'rocky steppe' area the medium was further impoverished by increasing the gravel to 25 per cent. Preliminary feeding consisted of hoof horn and bone meal, and this feeding was repeated four years later, when a thin layer of fine crushed granite was dug in across the site to make the soil structure even finer. 'No other fertilizer is applied; neither did we add manure or compost. Only delphiniums and lilies are helped with an annual feed.' The only mulch material used is gravel.

I have spelt all this out as Rosemarie Weisse explains, because the principles are so simple, so radical, so rewarding and therefore crying out to be put into practice. There is no intrinsic reason why spectacular flowering can only be achieved by piling on manure, if an equally beautiful and long-lasting effect can be achieved more economically and in more labour-saving ways.

One principle of such planting is understanding. Yet this does not depend on complicated book learning. Much of it is the understanding any gardener acquires who is attentive to whether plants are happy together; for in the end this is a matter of the purse, since unhappy plants will die and have to be replaced. The field that the town garden once was has long since been lost, and so any interested gardener is going to have to learn by trial and error what thrives in whose company, and whose company is not worth keeping. An old principle of gardening is that if your plant does not enjoy one position, try it somewhere else. By doing so we are actually trying to match it to something like conditions the plant – or its forebears – once knew in the wild.

Another principle is skill – knowing how much self-

This quiet, rich mosaic of plants, which includes alliums, grasses, scabious and asphodeline, thrives in impoverished, gravelly soil.

seeding to allow, when and how often to intervene and when to leave well alone. What is this, though, but hands-on experience? Gardeners are today learning how plants thrive simply with a mulch of gravel, and Rosemary Weisse's kind of planting extends the idea by thinking through the sorts of equable plant communities that can be created.

The principles must be adapted to local conditions, for what works in Munich's hot summers and cold winters will not do for softer littoral climates. But there is no reason, even in town gardens, why we could not think in terms that relate to hers. Woodland-edge conditions, after all, are what many town gardeners create, with light tree canopies and a mixture of sun and shade. We unconsciously emulate these conditions because they are ones in which good flowering plant communities are found. Deeper woodland has its floor of flowers and foliage, which can provide a model for those whose gardens offer deep shade from walls, trees and houses. Taking this further, to the ecologically minded, the most intractably water-logged corner in a corner can be a source of joy. 'Just think what you could grow there,' said a friend – providing of course that the water-logging is a constant.

Westpark shows that this style of planting can be as distinct and aesthetically pleasing as the herbaceous border. Rosemarie Weisse's example is a stimulating way forward, too, for gardeners who are conscious of the damage that human consumerism does to the natural landscape and its ecosystems, while lusting for a patch of garden to call their own. Many of us are going to look for garden perennials, for reasons reaching back into human history. We can match with our garden conditions plants whose original conditions in the wild come near them, particularly over the matter of light and shade, and we can often provide something like the drainage they would enjoy in their natural habitat. Such a thoughtful use of plant resources can leave both plants and human beings happy. An interested gardener is likely to acquire ecological habits of thought naturally.

Wolfgang Oehme and James van Sweden, the Offutt Garden

Rosemary Weisse's planting philosophy derives from Karl Foerster (1874–1970), the famous German gardener and nurseryman. So, too, does Wolfgang Oehme's, who studied horticulture and landscape architecture in postwar Germany. Oehme's planting design, like that found in Westpark and a number of other public gardens in Germany, is based on natural plant associations. Used sensitively and in conjunction with contours and landform, these associations bring an awareness of the wider landscape into the garden.

Foerster was keenly interested in grasses, and in the taller perennials and ferns, but for Oehme, moving to America, they became plants of especial significance because they belonged to an important part of the American landscape, the prairie. This hallmark of the Oehme and van Sweden partnership began to stand

ABOVE: Plants with prairie associations, such as calamogrostis, are prominent in Oehme and van Sweden's gardens. These large swatches and bands of planting are both sensuous and abstract.

LEFT: The ground plan of the Offutt Garden shows how the natural-looking planting emerges from extremely crisp built elements.

PERENNIALS
a. *Lythrum salicaria* 'Morden's Pink'
b. *Acanthus hungaricus*
c. *Ceratostigma plumbaginoides*
d. *Achillea filipendulina*
e. *Eupatorium purpureum* 'Gateway'
f. *Rudbeckia fulgida* 'Goldsturm'
g. *Yucca filamentosa*
h. *Hemerocallis* sp. (daylily)
i. *Sedum x telephium* 'Autumn Joy'
j. *Coreopsis verticillata* 'Moonbeam'

GRASSES & SEDGES
A. *Panicum virgatum* 'Haense Herms'
B. *Pennisetum orientale* (orient fountain grass)
C. *P. alopecuroides*
D. *Calamagrostis acutiflora stricta*
E. *Miscanthus sinensis gracillimus*

TREES & SHRUBS
1. *Crataegus phaenopyrum* (Washington hawthorn)
2. *Aralia spinosa* (Devil's-walking stick)
3. *Viburnum setigerum* (tea viburnum)
4. *V. rhytidophyllum* (leatherleaf viburnum)
5. *V. x pragense*

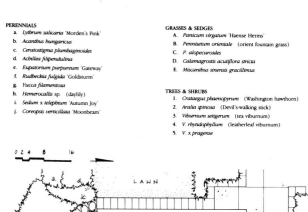

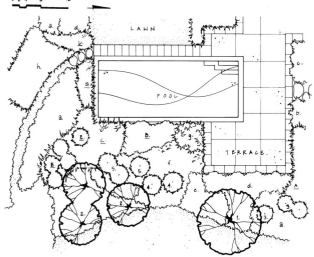

out from the time they were able to enlist the skills of Kurt Bluehmel in propagating the plants.

In the Offutt Garden grasses lead the eye out to the horizons, both echoing the contours of the land and visually breaking into them. They are as beautiful in winter as in summer. They accompany perennials such as Joe pye-weed, *Eupatorium purpureum* 'Gateway', which the partnership brought out of neglect. They soar above plants such as sedums and *Rudbeckia fulgida* var. *sullivantii* 'Goldsturm', that are planted over many square metres setting up ground planes that seem to weigh equally against distant fields and woods. A small number of varieties is used to cover large areas, yet there is no sense of impoverishment or

denial. It is sensuous, graceful and luxuriant. At the same time it is economical, for plants are simply left at the end of the year, to fall into new shapes and characters, a kind of canvas on which time and the season paints its own colours. They are cut down only at the beginning of spring. Such a garden is like an abstract painting.

The principles should work in different countries, including Britain, where they could create amazing changes in the relation between a garden and its natural surroundings, but they could not achieve the same grand effects of scale, and they would have to be realized in other media, for the grasses would not react so kindly to endless damp and they do not belong to the extent they do in America. To imagine Sissinghurst's orchard done in stipas and fountain grass shows how alien the effect could be. Yet the kind of planting suggests a new way of looking at gardens and landscape and at the relationship between them. Perhaps it has an analogy in those Dutch gardens where the perennials are allowed to stand after they have finished flowering, undergoing weird transformations of character.

Part of the magic of the Oehme and van Sweden gardens is that the hard landscaping, which is the responsibility of van Sweden, is hard-edged, a fact that emerges rather more from the plans than from photographs, where the crisp edges and level changes are only half-glimpsed through the soft crowds of stems and clouds of inflorescence. Whether the planting on its own could achieve the spatial quality that it does in conjunction with van Sweden's designs is doubtful. Contrast, although veiled, is as vital as ever. But the simplicity! An English border is always going to look voluble, complex and over-controlled by comparison.

Oehme and van Sweden's style is illustrated in another of their gardens by this pond-side planting of *Rudbeckia fulgida* var. *sullivantii* 'Goldsturm'. Plants and hard materials combine to give a magically simple reflection.

The Colour Tradition

THE POPES AT HADSPEN GARDEN, TON TER LINDEN AT RUINES, HOLLAND, THE WHITE GARDEN, SISSINGHURST, CHRISTOPHER LLOYD AT GREAT DIXTER

'Along bed with orange-scarlet, crimson, vermilion, salmon and magenta geraniums,' was what Russell Page once prescribed for a certain sunny spot near the house. Just saying the names of these different reds one after the other provides a kind of mental massage. Whether visual or verbal, colour is irresistible. But widely available bright colours are a relatively recent option.

Planting for colour goes back to the nineteenth century, when it arose partly as a consequence of the introduction of tender and semi-tropical plants from South America and South Africa. Their culture in Europe became possible as a result of greenhouse technology, cheap heating and cheap labour. With both flower and foliage providing lavish resources of colour, they led to the fashion for carpet bedding and bedding out which in 1901 Gertrude Jekyll describes as having swept, somewhat destructively, across Britain. In the late twentieth century we tend to recoil from the fulsomeness of the schemes. Perhaps at the time there was something 'great' about the decision to use colour so boldly and in such large masses; though the bluish light of northern Europe is scarcely the most sympathetic ambience for hot, strong colours, unless they are eased carefully into the garden landscape.

To anticipate for a moment, the style receives a sort of transformation in some of the mid-twentieth-century work of Roberto Burle Marx, the Brazilian landscape gardener who died in 1994. Using his native plants, many of which are related to those used by the Victorians, he took them around in great swirling patterns, creating a kind of abstract art on the ground. The success of such planting depends on the strong light of Brazil and the way in which the patterns are contained

GARDEN by ROBERTO BURLE MARX

Burle Marx's bold use of large zones of colour in abstract shapes brought new dimensions to plans, as to the gardens themselves. Work such as this has profoundly influenced Preben Jakobsen's thinking (see page 131).

by the powerful forest landscape that surrounds the sites. Some say such schemes look better in his beautiful plans – which really are abstract paintings – than on the ground.

Back in the nineteenth century, bright colour entered society in other ways. Many new, chemically based pigments began to be manufactured. Colour theory flourished. By the 1860s Decaisne and Naudin in their four-volume *Manuel de l'amateur des jardins* are telling their readers about the Chevreul colour wheel and how pairs of complementary colours, such as purple and yellow, can enhance one another. In painting the Impressionists gave colour a new importance, and, of course, colour and flowers come together in Monet's garden at Giverny (see page 56) as well as in his paintings.

In England Gertrude Jekyll's own colour gardening was a revelation for those who saw it. *Colour in the Flower Garden* in particular explained her principles. There she describes the way in which, in her main border, grey and blue were allowed to saturate the eye, which then passed 'with extraordinary avidity' to the succeeding yellows. After an interlude where they were intermingled with reds and clarets, the yellows emerged on their own again. Once more the eye became saturated with a single colour and once more turned with appetite to the complementary greys and purples, which appeared especially brilliant because of the preparation it had received. An invaluable way of learning about colour in the garden is to carry out just such an experiment, even though it may be on a small scale and involve moving around plants in their containers.

One gardener who, says Andrew Lawson, followed her colour principles to the letter was Peter Healing. He wrote most vividly about his garden at the Priory, Kemerton, Gloucester, in *The Englishman's Garden*. The main border, an astonishing 46m (150ft) long and 5.5m (18ft) wide, 'was planned to start with grey foliage through white, cream and pink to pale yellow, working up by strong yellows to a crescendo of reds, maroon and

Peter Healing, taking his cue from Gertrude Jekyll, experimented with the hot, powerful colours provided by kniphofias, dahlias, nicotiana and red-veined chard.

bronze. From there it would fade gradually in the reverse order down to whites and greys in the far distance.' Much more colour planting followed!

Peter Healing was doing something out of the ordinary in going for a red border, for most gardeners have preferred paler lilacs, mauves, and pinks – colours that Gertrude Jekyll used to perfection but that also interact well with soft, hazy light. You also can't go far wrong with them. In colour gardening the stakes are high, for the whole thing can easily topple over into colour chaos. But if you are successful the results provide an astonishing emotional feast. Some of the more daring colour experiments are, interestingly, carried out by gardeners with a special expertise, either from painting or from colour psychology – and, of course, to be a skilled horticulturist and plant propagator is a great asset. One successful set of experiments is to be found in the gardening of a young Canadian couple, Sandra and Nori Pope, at Hadspen Garden near Castle Cary in Somerset.

The Popes at Hadspen Garden

The garden lies facing the sun below a magnificently wooded combe. Once upon a time it was Penelope Hobhouse's, but after she left at the end of the 1970s, it was neglected and in garden terms became ruinous. The Popes have been reclaiming and developing the 2.2 hectares (5½ acres) since 1987. They love the English gardening scene but gently remark on our obsession with the past and dare to think that gardening can benefit from coming into contact with fresh ideas. 'Thinking – and thinking your way through to understanding – is really fun.' And colour is the idea that the two of them are taking as far as it will go.

Nori has a long-standing interest in how we perceive colour: how, for example, exposure to one colour can make us see its complementary. It has even been suggested, for instance, that Matisse, who had a studio with grey walls, was stimulated to paint *The Red Studio* because coming in from the garden's intense green left him with a vivid red after-image. Nori and Sandra Pope choose to carry out colour experiments with plants instead of paints. Can you, for example, intensify a monochrome sensation in your planting by adding touches of its complementary? Most of us tend to tone down strong colour effects, opting for the 'tasteful', but another way is to increase the tension, to 'get the visual synapses really snapping'. Why recreate the monotones of our everyday lives? In Hadspen Garden the Popes are playing with perception and creating stunning colour borders.

Hadspen Garden has a remarkable feature that encourages them in their experiments: an enclosed garden with a kilometre (1090 yards) of curved wall. This

This is perhaps more successful than the Priory red border because planting here explores a narrow range of colours (from left to right): *Helenium* 'Moerheim Beauty', *Phormium tenax*, *Crocosmia* 'Lucifer' and *Dahlia* 'Ellen Houston'. Serendipity: nasturtiums happily mound the wall behind.

OPPOSITE: The success of this view depends on the planting's complete simplicity. The cloudy blue-purple of *Nepeta* 'Six Hills Giant' also suggests distance.

RIGHT: Very satisfying effects can be gained from the play of different kinds of yellow, here provided by lupins, anthemis and achillea, supported by yellow-tinged foliage.

was probably built to deflect cold air rolling off the slopes in frosty weather, but it also echoes the bowl shape of the hills most attractively. Even in itself this curve suggests movement, particularly as it is on a sloping hillside, and the Popes' planting exploits this. The border against the wall consists of a series of monochrome plantings, where the visitor follows the rhythm of colour changes, from stronger, more saturated, colours on the upper part of the curve, down to pastel tones and white below. This sequence is practical because the top section gets full sun, appropriate for the sun-loving plants among which there are strong yellows, oranges and reds, while the lower part of the curve is shadier, suiting paler tones.

Where the brick of the old wall is reddish, the Popes plant their reds and oranges and crimsons. As the brick colour changes to purplish, the fortuitous result of some re-building in the past, so they develop blue and purple zones. Starting by focusing on a particular colour, the Popes think through their planting in terms of rhythm, shape and texture: 'moundy things' are contrasted with tall clumps, and spikes and spires; the sword-like stems of *Crocosmia* 'Lucifer' with the softer body of *Dahlia* 'Bishop of Llandaff'. Towards the back of this same bed in June and July, red sweet peas are lifted skywards on a tripod made of hazel wands. Orange-red nasturtiums manage to climb up the wall. The eye is taken upwards by *Leonitus nepetifolia* with its copper whorls. Large leaves are provided by dusky canna lilies.

The Popes have an outstanding repertoire of plants. They can plant so that colour in a border is not for a week or a month, but carries on with modulations from spring to autumn. This is immensely original, a far cry from the Jekyll colour border that was planned to be the highlight of a particular season. At the same time that some of the plants are unusual, others are so common that visitors sometimes fail to recognize them in such an exotic context. A strong orange-red sits in front of the 'Bishop of Llandaff': you blink before you

1. **ENTRANCE & POTTING SHED GARDEN**
2. **PEACH WALK**
3. **TEAHOUSE GARDEN**
4. **LILY POND BORDER**
5. **CURVED BORDER**
6. **YELLOW BORDER**
7. **HYDRANGEA BORDER**
8. **PLUM/GREY BORDER**

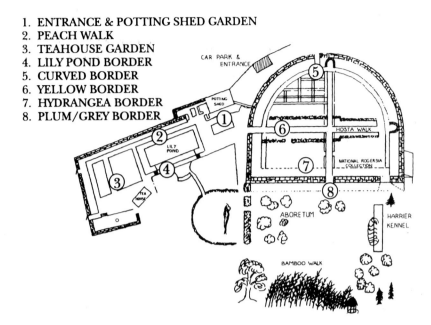

Plan of Hadspen Garden, showing the huge curved walls (right) and calm centre with large pond (left).

realize this colour experience is provided by the common marigold, *Tagetes patula* species. Brilliant red salvias, *Salvia fulgens*, are found here, too. Earlier in the year *Euphorbia griffithii* 'Dixter' brings in its strong soft orange-red. By June *Atriplex hortensis* var. *rubra*, the ruby-leaved sorrel, is threading its way right across the border.

Nori enjoys intensifying the monochromes. Sandra thinks about links through a section, and between sections. To achieve a smooth transition she brings neighbouring colours across, so that the reds ease off into the muted oranges and dark brown velvets of a sunflower, *Helianthus* 'Velvet Queen'. Between red and blue, she will weave mauves and violets.

To have to take in these plantings at one go would be overwhelming; but you don't, because of the slope and curve, and the rhythm of your own walking. Plants also sometimes create screens. Across the path from where the colour is concentrated, is 'a sort of moving curtain' of *Verbena bonariensis* that half-promises a view of what it hides. Originally the

verbena belonged to the colour border, but then it walked over to join red beet in the vegetable garden. The Popes are happy with such accidents that occur over time, and count them rightly as part of the experimentation. Although they do not borrow Gilles Clément's phrase, a Garden of Movement, like him they allow events to occur in their garden. Some degree of experience is needed to let these happenstance plant migrations and self-seedings occur, but there is no reason why more gardens should not allow such effects. Where you are lucky enough to have the space, self-seeding, used selectively, leads to wonderful effects both from the sheer mass that can develop and from the random touches of colour, like touches of paint. Ton ter Linden, whose garden is described on page 102, calls the gardener's work with self-seeders 'creative weeding'. *Milium effusum* 'Aureum', Bowles's gold grass, and the golden feverfew, are two plants that, like *Verbena bonariensis*, one can move around, taking them out where they fall in the wrong place, but effectively painting with them.

Round and down the slope Nori is planning a section in chartreuse and violet. There will be tall wispy plants at the front, like the verbena which will provide some of the violet, while more solid plants will be planted further back.

There are various colour areas away from the curved wall. A long axial walk leading to the gate to the field beyond is planted with *Nepeta* 'Six Hills Giant', because the cloudy blue leads into the distance. This catmint is complemented by the warm yellow shingle, as ever a sympathetic medium.

At right angles to this walk there is a wide double border, which investigates yellow. Here there is play between the 'out of focus' foliage of fennel and the sharply cut forms of yellow iris flowers and leaves. To encourage the eye to see the border's colour even more intensely, Nori lets in small touches of blue, such as the forget-me-not flowers of brunnera in the spring and aconites in the autumn. On one side of the path this border is in full sun, and the Popes saturate our eye with colour. On the other side, where a beech hedge backing the border casts shade, they choose paler yellows, even drifting off into a mass of white epilobium, *Epilobium angustifolium* var. *album*, a desirable relative of the common willow herb that was highly praised by Gertrude Jekyll.

Everywhere the eye is encouraged to move on by the rhythmical patterning in these long beds. The Popes observe the way that different shapes affect the progress of their visitors. A great mound on a corner brings us to a halt. Where plant shapes are misty and moving in the wind, people move on. At the top of the yellow border, a seedling of *Paulownia tomentosa* planted itself – a perfect end-of-border stop to slow down the visitor. It is constantly pruned because it wants to turn into the tall tree its genes destined it to be; pruning stimulates huge juvenile growth.

There is one more colour garden. In a small walled enclosure towards the house they are trying out blues and whites. Here the feeling is stiller, and the place is cool and contemplative. *Lathyrus sativus* is taken through love-in-a-mist, *Nigella damascena*, like a thread through a piece of material. But it is a hard scheme to bring off on a large scale because the almost cerulean blues of some of the salvias and the clear blue of *Omphalodes cappadocica*, of the ceanothuses and of *Delphinium* 'Alice Artindale' do not interact with the far commoner purple-blues of aconites and columbines or even the bluest aster. An original solution to the problem is found in the blue garden at Parc André-Citroën, down the path from Gilles Clément's Garden of Movement. Here there is a vast Persian carpet filled with greys, lavenders, purplish salvias and thymes. In an adjacent, separate square, utterly blue delphiniums are mixed with the inky indigos and near blacks of irises and lupins. You feel that you are seeing blue for the first time.

When the Popes mention a painter to compare with their gardening experiments, it is not one of the French colourists but the action painter Jackson Pollock, who, when he had an idea, set out to see where his paint spills led him. The Popes do not control their schemes by working out their plans on paper beforehand. Throughout the summer Sandra makes copious notes on heights, shapes and colour mixes, and then plants out of a mixture of experience and intuition. Both are totally unprescriptive about working with colour, feeling there is no set way. They originally intended to plant out the full colour spectrum, but then realized they would simply end up with a colour chart in flowers, a curiosity rather than a good visual experience. The point about your garden, they say, is that it is going to be your personal expression; if you want to be hemmed in by rules and recipes, that, too, is a personal expression.

Like Beth Chatto – and Peter Healing – they resort readily to the language of music to describe their gardening. They are aware that the eye has difficulties in 'following a non-rhythmic painting'; so they make the most of the rhythmic qualities of plants. Hadspen House garden does not display static showpieces but unfolds colour experiences that modulate as the season progresses. At the same time, while some areas may seem to be a romantic tangle there is an underlying order, the continuing exposition of an idea that the gardeners are at pains to carry through

I think the woodland background of the colour plantings contributes to their success. There is room for the colours to breathe. There is contrast, too. Around the massive tank with the hillside rising steeply above it, everything is quieter. Here there is more emphasis on plant shapes, whether a great clump of the grass, *Miscanthus sinensis*, down by the water or the spiky giant rosette of the cardoon's great grey leaves. And if there were not this large peaceful oasis at the centre, I doubt if the garden would be quite so wonderful.

Ton ter Linden at Ruines, Holland

Sandra and Nori Pope say they were galvanized into colour experiments by Ton ter Linden's garden. Ton is a painter who, starting from a neglected meadow and some dilapidated farm buildings, has made an outstanding garden in this village in northern Holland. Unlike the Popes, he turned to the Impressionists for inspiration

The emotionally charged planting in Ton ter Linden's garden could be compared with that of the Cottage Garden at Sissinghurst, but it is more painterly and concerned with veils of colour. Artemisia provides a shock of cold against the orange alstroemeria.

and aims to create effects of 'nature, light and atmosphere'. At the same time he has a strong feeling for indigenous plants, rejecting the use of exotics that do not blend into the flat, domestic Dutch landscape.

Ton and his partner Anne first had to plant trees to provide windbreaks. Hedges gave further protection and also were the means to create a series of enclosed gardens. With the green walls established, Ton began his paintings. They are remarkable. Take the July one in orange. The visitor approaches it under the quiet green of an old apple tree and then, turning a corner, is likely to be brought to a halt by two tall borders between yew hedges. There is a fantastic weaving going on, in which

Ton manages to respect the growth habits of the plants while doing the most extraordinary things with colour. Warm orange is dominant, taken by alstroemerias here and there through the borders. These edge up against the mahogany red of *Helenium* 'Moerheim Beauty' and masses of yellow from achilleas, more heleniums and tall spires of verbascum. What is exciting is how the cold grey of artemisias, such as *Artemisia ludoviciana*, runs through the warm orange-reds, which are challenged here and there by the purple-leaved sorrel, touches of the crimson loosestrife and a scattering of scarlet dahlias.

The heights of plants immediately next to the grass path between the two borders are greater than conventional gardening wisdom might suggest. Immediately the plants come closer to you. Towards the back of the borders, heights increase until the pale coral plumes of *Macleaya cordata* float above the yew hedge. The planting plans Ton provides look straightforward enough, but the gardening that allows and encourages all this to happen is highly skilled. It is a tactile sort of gardening – you know that hands have recently been at work, shaping, encouraging and restraining – and it is high risk gardening, close to toppling into disorder, which again makes for excitement. Colour risks accompany gardening risks, and because the colours are framed by the precisely trimmed greenery of the hedges, walking between these borders is like walking into a painting.

Ton ter Linden describes his planting in terms of proportion, line and rhythm, and in more original ways:

The use of slender high plants gives the border an appearance of transparency. The light dives into the sea of flowers, and nowhere is it stopped by a massive, closed surface of colour. You will never find sharply framed blocks of colour next to each other, but you will discover the next colour in the previous one.

Colours are 'bound and extinguished' by the silver grey of artemisias, which are a leitmotif throughout.

There is a blue garden, a white garden, which peaks

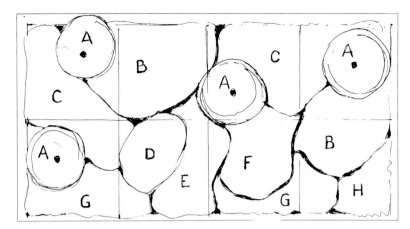

ABOVE: A sample planting by Ton ter Linden, blending *Rosa* 'Golden Wings' (A), *Alchemilla mollis* (B), *Lysimachia ciliata* (C), *Hemerocallis citrina* (D), *Nicotiana langsdorffii* (E), *Nicotiana* 'Lime Green' (F), *Limnanthes douglasii* (G) and *Ruta graveolens* (H).

OVERLEAF: This is a wonderful study in whites, greys and greens, tended with a skilful hand. Sissinghurst's White Garden looks almost contrived by comparison.

in June, and a 'sun border' of many colours, which peaks in July. Between all these are calm interludes of grass, or a seat or two under a group of little lime trees. As each of these gardens passes its peak, it is not tidied away. Instead, flowers and stems are allowed to stand till late in the year, undergoing all sorts of transformations, not only of colour, but of mood and character. This kind of autumnal beauty, close to wildness, seems to be a characteristic of Dutch gardeners who 'play with nature'.

A risk of colour gardening is that it leads us to undervalue the equally beautiful but quieter colours that can be found in woodland and gardens from November to February. This is, after all, where the great begetter of the colour theme, Gertrude Jekyll, began her colour musings in *Wood and Garden*. The Dutch garden is a reminder of this other world. So, too, is Beth Chatto's gravel garden where, come the autumn, she only deadheads the dying plants selectively. As late as February, tawny and hay-coloured grass stems enrich the brown-green of bergenias with coral and burgundy tints.

The White Garden, Sissinghurst

Gertrude Jekyll expressed interest in single-colour gardens, and Edith Wharton made a white garden at The Mount at Lenox, but the person who put the white garden on the map was Vita Sackville-West. Since her creation began to be seen by visitors in the early 1950s, a white garden has become an especially prized form of planting. I have, in truth, often been disappointed by them and would like to revisit the most famous of them all to see what it is about the Sissinghurst planting that lifts it into the realm of the great.

'It may be a terrible failure,' said Vita Sackville-West of the white, grey and green garden she was planning to make. 'I only want to suggest that such experiments are worth trying.' She and Harold Nicolson were always experimenting with the Sissinghurst sampler. Here she put in a purple panel, there one of sunset colours, one of rose-shaded pinks and mauves, and several green panels, including the softer green of the orchard. Dark stitching of yew marked boundaries. These are like an accentuation of the hedges dividing the coverlet of the Kentish countryside seen from the tower, with its fields, copses and oast-houses.

The metaphor of a fabric easily springs to mind with the White Garden. Many years ago Anne Scott-James, in *Sissinghurst: The Making of a Garden* (1974), wrote of the skill with which 'the pattern of grey and green foliage plants is woven'. The various textures of the

The White Garden is actually rich in colours – the bluish *Hosta sieboldiana* var. *elegans*, for example – to which white flowers, such as the sidalcea, are a highlight.

planting are completely distinct. There are the curves of hosta leaves against the vertical hatching of ballotas and the little dashes of the flowers of lambs' ears, *Stachys byzantina* (formerly called *S. lanata*): chain stitches, cross stitches, stem stitches, not to mention leaf stitches. Satiny flower petals stand out against grey foliage that, because of its maritime and Mediterranean origins, comes equipped with hairy or glaucous or leathery leaves. The flowers look like fine silken embroidery on a coarser wool or cotton ground. The White Garden is a sampler within a sampler, subdivided by the stitching of those little squared-off box hedges. Their needlework is fine indeed, especially next to the old bricks laid in basket-weave pattern.

Entering from the lawn below the tower, all around is not so much white and green as a study in close tonal

ABOVE: Textures here are beautifully abstract and complementary: 'white' is a misnomer for what is a subtle study in greens and greys (artemisia and, by the gate, rodgersia).

OPPOSITE: Structure and chiaroscuro contrasts are vital to the success of the White Garden. The arbour of *Rosa longicuspis* gives the little garden a still centre.

harmonies, like one of Whistler's paintings. Tone refers to the amount of light or dark in a colour, and the distinctive sort of leaf here is one in which there is a lot of white. Not all the leaves are the same whitish-grey. The silver-grey of *Cineraria maritima* makes the grey-green of *Artemisia pontica*, Roman wormwood, look darker, almost slightly dirty, by comparison and the latter makes its cleaner neighbours gleam all the more. The foliage of *Artemisia ludoviciana* is a fraction lighter

than that of lambs' ears, *Stachys byzantina*, and the stachys leaves are lighter than those of the *Hydrangea quercifolia* next to them.

It is because tones are, typically, so close to one another that the stitches, that is to say the plant textures, can stand out so distinctly. In much of this garden, the eye has little work to do in distinguishing sharp contrasts of tone and so is more alert to textural changes. The planting is great partly because these are so wonderfully exploited and partly because it makes so much out of what sounds like a minimalist idea.

But if all the tones were merely pale, how pallid would the White Garden be! Visitors know how refreshing it is on a hot day, how welcome is the deep shade under the *Rosa longicuspis* arbour and how cleansing the contrasts of green and white are in the eastern part of the garden where box hedging encloses 'Iceberg' roses or *Lilium candidum* or, in May, 'White Triumphator' tulips. Yet moving away from the areas where the garden is shady, green and oasis-like, out into the sun, the experience the garden offers is far from ghostly and bleached. This is because there is actually so much colour in the foliage. The pale tones are tinted blue, green, white and even yellow. *Ruta graveolens*, *Artemisia abrotanum* (lad's love), *Salvia argentea*, *Hosta plantaginea*: such a range of leaves suffuses the rise and fall of the planting with colour.

The other feature of the planting is that it works by contrasts, calm and undistracting though they be. Whites and greys and greens with a little yellow in them edge up against those towards the cold end of the spectrum. *Artemisia ludoviciana* is one of the most silvery of greys, but in this garden it is next to a cloud of *Gillenia trifoliata* whose white flowers look flushed with pink because of its reddish calyces and stems. The dead white of *Lychnis coronaria* 'Alba' is seen against the tints of *Lupinus microphyllus* 'Noble Maiden'. The play of warm and cool is a recurrent effect in the garden, even in zones where green becomes fuller and richer. The leaves of *Zantedeschia aethiopica*

'Crowborough' positively glow in front of the bloodless grey of *Macleaya cordata*.

The White Garden's foliage is thus an enchanting play between warmer and cooler, and the white admixed with so much of it only serves to reveal how much colour actually rests in many of the leaves. The same is true of all the flowers, which as Gertrude Jekyll said of white flowers in *Wood and Garden*, are scarcely ever pure white. Nearly always there is a trace of cream or buff or pink in them. Dead white is a rare experience in this garden; the blossoms of *Rosa longicuspis*, hinting at cream, are a more typical version of white. So the balance even among colours described as 'white' is tipped to warmer rather than cooler, and this is partly what creates a recurrent glow across the little garden.

In the green of the box hedging, as well as in the dull reddish brick paths, there is a lot of yellow. Light off this reflects on to the plant embroidery, which at the same time stands out against the deep blackish-green of the yew hedges. In colour, as in tone, everything depends on relationship. The contrasts here are so active and so thought-through that they make the place full of life, even before one adds in the bold character of so many of the plants: *Crambe cordifolia*, implausibly vast, *Paeonia suffruticosa*, impossibly extravagant, not to mention ostrich ferns, *Matteuccia struthiopteris*, unbelievably tight coiled.

The White Garden, the most subtly woven and embroidered panel in the Sissinghurst sampler, has also become its most renowned experiment, treasured especially for the way it glows as light fades. It is an entertaining thought that, while thoroughly innocuous, these delicate stitches have also proved somewhat subversive. For, while antiquated laws prevented Vita Sackville-West from inheriting Knole because she was a woman, her inventive plant weaving and embroidery has brought her more fame than she would ever have received as inheritor of the ancestral home. Who would have thought that great planting could be so powerful?

Christopher Lloyd at Great Dixter

A risk of colour gardening is that it leads to the neglect of structure. The tulips at Great Dixter display both their gardener's colour sense and his appreciation of their noble form.

Great Dixter's porch is shady. A pot of 'Halcro' tulips by the door is cooled down by pink stocks and hyacinths. But to the side, towards the sunken garden, there is a complete contrast. A curved bed at the edge of the lawn in the sun is crammed with wallflowers, 'Primrose Bedder', 'Ivory White' and 'Fire Queen'. May wallflowers are an old cottage-garden theme but to mass and concentrate them in this way, without any distraction, is highly original and shows enormous confidence. They are slabs of colour pouring forwards and held in check only by the trim green curve of the lawn.

In themselves they lack rhythm, and this is brought to the planting by blocks of tulips planted behind them. They are 'White Triumphator', 'Greuze' and 'Westpoint'. Near *Tulipa* 'Greuze' is a huge *Erysimum* (*Cheiranthus*) 'Bowles' Mauve', purples made all the more purple for being set against their complementary colour, yellow. Is this planting more remarkable for its swagger or for its control? That the show is so eye-catching and pleasing depends on the restraint shown elsewhere. The background foliage is dark and quiet. The pinkish brick of the old farm buildings may contain the flower colours, but they are muffled. So the bright colours leap out as a greeting.

The display sets up a theme of excitement and order that runs through the rest of the garden. In the west-facing long border tulips dance along, their colours constantly interacting with the dark yew hedges behind them. Here the parrot tulip 'Orange Favourite' circles a golden elder, while perennial honesty, *Lunaria rediviva*, stops the colours becoming too rich and glutinous. Further along the tentative warmth of Dixon's golden elm coming into leaf is brought out by drifts of yellow-

Christopher Lloyd changes his tulip colour schemes from year to year. His good eye ensures that the colours in the border enhance each other.

bronze tulips, such as 'Absolon'. New foliage on a purple cotinus accents the bronze stripes and streaks of old cottage tulips that look like mixtures of marmalade and lemons. They stand above forget-me-nots, so that orange and blue complementaries activate one another. There is no distraction encountered here from mauve or violet. Tulips along here fit into a space that is already

well defined by the yew tree walls, and underscore the theme of shapeliness further forward in the border.

Up in the raised garden, formerly the old kitchen garden, Christopher Lloyd abandons the yellows and oranges and plants red 'Halcro' tulips. Looking down the path their crispness again echoes that of the yew hedge, and their hard, clear colour is softened by the rufous stems of *Fuchsia magellanica* 'Riccartonii'. Looking up the path, 'Halcro' emerges out of young lupin foliage. The red and green pull equally strongly and so does the patterning both of red flowers and green lupin leaves.

But we also see the tulips against *Hebe* 'Pewter Dome' and the 'comfortable dumpling', as Christopher Lloyd puts it in his catalogue, of *H. cupressoides* 'Boughton Dome'. Such crisp lines and profiles would be too formal for the cottagey corner that waved 'welcome', but are just right at this point where York stone paths cross. The stone's neutral tones anchor the strong red. How less effective 'Halcro' would be here if it were placed against a green lawn. Instead all the various greens of the hebes ease it into its setting, while on the other side of the path crossing, it is softened by *Euphorbia griffithii* 'Dixter', angelica and the pale yellow flowers of *Prunus laurocerasus* 'Otto Luyken'.

Tulips go well with formal geometry, whether it is provided by a yew hedge at Great Dixter or an urn, 2m (more than 6ft) wide, at the entrance to Brooklyn Botanic Garden, another place where the colour rhythms they set up are wonderfully exploited. They also create formal geometry. In large, simple cylindrical planters, one colour per planter, they can dramatically bring form into even a small back garden. But in the Sussex countryside to depart from the classic dark reds that match the yew so perfectly into clamorous orange and yellow is quite unexpected and pure genius.

Beyond *Tulipa* 'Halcro' the browny stems of *Fuchsia magellanica* 'Riccartonii' nicely recede from us towards the bluish distance.

Large Leafists

MYLES CHALLIS IN LONDON, RICHARD PARTRIDGE IN LONDON,
ERIC OSSART AT CHAUMONT-SUR-LOIRE

Large leaves are amazing and mysterious. They can turn the world into a wonderland in which we suddenly become rather small, peering up instead of looking down, as we are accustomed. They can – as in the case of the Brazilian *Gunnera manicata* – leave us standing in a watery green light, as though we had strayed into a remarkable green room or had suddenly changed our element. They can make us feel we have wandered into a surrealist world of dreams. Nose to nose with a large leaf – of *Tetrapanax papyrifer*, say – you can imagine you are transported to the world of leaves. They can put us in contact with primitive sensations at the same time as their visual qualities are so sophisticated. Equally remarkable is the character that

Gunnera manicata creates a green room.

the novelist Paul Scott saw in leaves in the jungle: their textures, that 'communicate themselves through sight to imaginary touch, exciting the finger-tips'.

When I began making gardens in the 1960s, the large-leaf factor never crossed my mind. I didn't like the odd hosta I saw, I loathed bergenias, and didn't know of the existence of the wild verbascum, *Verbascum bombyciferum*, used at Denmans to such good effect. I remember it was one of the famous Beth Chatto Chelsea exhibits that made me notice the leaf of *V. olympicum*. After I became more involved with plants, and had been ticked off by a skilled garden-designer for thinking of them as individuals instead of seeing them together, my eyes gradually opened. I began to notice the blue-leaved hostas at Sissinghurst, and their effect on the planting around them.

I imagine the story of how large-leaf consciousness dawned on me is shared by many gardeners. Nowadays not only are there wonderful hosta nurseries, which offer some of the best new hosta hybrids from America. The designers are to hand saying 'Look at the wonderful calming influence of large leaves in a garden'. There are excellent books on foliage in general and architectural foliage in particular.

At the same time a new note has entered the scene. It involves a revival of tropical plants grown by the Victorians in their large greenhouses, and selections from them that may withstand a mild winter. The agents of change have been, in particular, a designer, Myles Challis, and a specialist nursery, Architectural Plants. Even if some of their ideas involve resources in over-wintering that most of us cannot provide, the garden of Richard Partridge will show how, by a sensible selection, the aesthetic can be carried into the suburbs.

Myles Challis in London

Stepping into this little shoe-box of a garden, 12 x 6m (40 x 20ft), off the London street, the experience is so exotic as to seem surreal. There are tall bamboo leaves and the huge wind sails of *Ensete ventricosum*, the Abyssinian banana. Shoulder high there are *Gunnera manicata*, aralias, and the tall flowers of *Acanthus*

Paulownia imperialis, pruned yearly, produces monster junior growth. Dark-leaved canna provide more detailed interest for the visitor.

mollis (bear's breeches). A little nearer the ground there are the leaves of *Cotinus* 'Grace', *Hosta* 'Zounds' and *H.* 'Sum and Substance', melianthus, purple-leaved canna lilies and *Phormium* 'Dark Delight'. Hugging the ground more closely are hostas such as *H. sieboldiana* var. *elegans*, and *Polystichum setiferum* 'Divisilobum' (the soft shield fern).

The plants here create mystery. You do not know what lies before you as you grope your way forwards, adjusting to scale and extremes of shade and light, as well as the wonder of it all. In fact, a small path turns out to lead to a pond, where a vast stone fountain face

upon layer. The huge palmate foliage of the rice paper plant interleaves with the fronds of *Dicksonia antarctica*, and both are shaded by a canopy further above.

Myles's intentions have been crystal clear. Falling in love with jungle foliage at an early age, and by chance having the means to grow it, he has sought to create it in his town garden, ever increasing the interest. Nowadays there are injections of colour from plants such as canna lilies, whose leaves ensure that the huge vermilion inflorescence is absorbed into the planes and textures around it.

If the garden has to be dismantled in winter, and stored in the greenhouses of friends, this one flaw must be forgiven because of the extreme generosity and flair of what it can put on show in the growing season.

ABOVE: The vast leaves of *Ensete ventricosum* offer a surreal canopy to the visitor and a percussive sound-track too.
RIGHT: We would not be able to appreciate the vast leaves without Myles Challis's well-thought out path, which snakes through the garden.

is half screened by equally vast leaves. The dream atmosphere is increased by the rattle of bamboo and banana leaves overhead.

This garden is simply a *tour de force*. It serves, among other things, to illustrate Christopher Tunnard's remark in *Gardens in the Modern Landscape* (1938) that 'a garden as a work of art is only natural in relation to its materials; it is a product of the imagination'. Yet it does not browbeat the visitor, because its qualities are so sensory and calming. It is in the highest degree rewarding in terms of texture, shape and pattern. And such formal categories do not match the wonderful effect of scale and the play of light and shade over all the surfaces. The canopies build layer

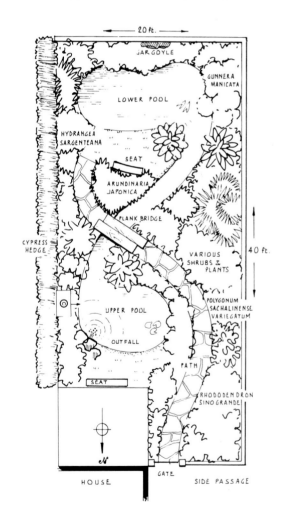

Richard Partridge in London

Richard Partridge has created a green mysterious garden behind a semi-detached house on a steep south-facing slope in north London. The size is 24.2m (80ft) by 9.1m (30ft). From the moment you step out from the back of the house, there are glimpses upwards of all sorts of lines and leaves and patches of light and shade. *Mahonia lomariifolia* towers above you, ending in wheels of spiky leaves etched black against the light. On the bank leading away from the house a rhododendron has been pruned to grow into a small tree, its trunk sinuous and rich-textured. You wonder if, like Alice in Wonderland, you have suddenly shrunk. If you happen to look down there is a magnificent carpeting of *Bergenia ciliata*, whose leaves here are outsize.

Narrow steps rise to a sun terrace paved in York

In Richard Partridge's garden this path leading to the mysteries beyond is well framed by a tree trunk. The spiky fan-leaves of *Chamaerops humilis* integrate well with their surroundings.

stone. To reach it you pass under a *Tetrapanax papyrifer*, the rice-paper plant, related to the fatsia and with leaves of the same shape, but often 46cm (18in) across, a mysterious matt green, with undersides and stems covered in pale brown indumentum. Around this terrace there are all manner of shades and tints of green: *Melianthus major* like a fountain in front of the pallid vegetation of *Acer negundo* 'Flamingo', and behind that again the spikes of a massive *Phormium tenax*. Tree peony foliage, soft green, *Zantedeschia aethiopica* 'Green Goddess', whose leaves are matt and larger than those of the type species, the velvety texture of a large patch of *Geranium renardii* – these are just some of the leaves providing shape and colour to flow around the little sitting area.

The steps entice you further up the hill, past a huge *Crambe cordifolia*, *Hydrangea aspera* 'Villosa' and *H. quercifolia*. It feels like woodland. There are ferns, rodgersias, a *Daphniphyllum macropodum*, *Corylus maxima* 'Purpurea' (the purple hazel nut), alongside *Viburnum cinnamomifolium*, whose leaves are like

The foliage of *Cotinus coggyria* 'Grace' and tetrapanax is all the more beautiful for being planted so that we see light filtering through it.

those of *V. davidii* but larger. The boundaries of the garden have disappeared behind dense but lucid planting of shrubs and small trees.

Unexpectedly at the top, you emerge on to a second terrace the width of the garden where at one end is a pond, flanked by inulas, rodgersias, a gunnera, as well as delicate ferns, including the purple-stemmed form of the royal fern, *Osmunda regalis* ssp. *purpurascens*. Planting on the north boundary includes a tulip tree and a giant-leaved rhododendron, *R. sinogrande*. *Hosta* 'Frances Williams Improved' keeps up the large leaf theme at ground level.

It is one of those gardens where, retracing your steps, you seem to be in a new landscape because all the plants fall into a new relationship. Going up hill you entered foresty depths; coming down is like looking across a hillside in some country where all the plants have dramatic shapes.

How, as a friend said, did Richard ever manage to imagine such a garden, the only garden he has ever had? What he found thirty years ago was a cement path all round, two cement circles each with a standard rose at its centre, and two small lawns. After a preliminary herbaceous phase ('mildewed asters'), he made a collection of green flowers (some still survive). Then he read Margery Fish's books and went in for ground

cover, which he found unsatisfactory because two-dimensional. His catalogue education made a quantum leap forward when he acquired a copy of Graham Stuart Thomas's *The Modern Florilegium* with its emphasis on plants of good form and foliage. Then in the mid-1970s he read an article in a Sunday paper called 'The New Gardening': 'stop bothering with herbaceous borders and lawns, and instead go for foliage interest, plant associations and the pleasures of plant form.' This activated Richard's memories of the Cameroon rain forest, where he had once worked, and around 1975 he visited the famous Jardin exotique in Morocco, north of Rabat. Here you first see the garden from rope ladders between trees before getting down among the plants. In the mid-1980s, by which time most of the present lay-out was in place, he met Myles Challis. Myles said: 'You must grow your ligularias, *Peltiphyllum peltatum* and the invasive petasites round a pond.' So the modest pond came into existence and made local frogs happy, as well as the giant-leaved inulas.

Thus the clear intentions evident today in Richard's gardening have arisen from a visionary memory of jungle, whose realization was made possible by his gradual self-education in matters of foliage, good horticulture and his wish to make a mysterious green garden that gave up its secrets bit by bit. He wanted to create the illusion of space where in reality there was very little.

Today he would say his principles are never to grow a plant with insignificant foliage, always to choose plants that make a good gesture and, as far as humanly possible – for like the rest of us he suffers from plant greed – to give each plant enough space to reveal its habit of growth. Of course he makes exceptions, such as pale lilac phlox, painting the shade in which it stands, because although its foliage is nothing to speak of its scent evokes his childhood.

Clearly he thinks in terms of different levels and canopies. He invites your eye to explore pattern and colour at ground level, but then takes it up and around. Golden feverfew gives way to the foliage of *Cimicifuga simplex* 'Atropurpurea', behind which is a small *Aesculus pavia*, then *Inula magnifica* and above that the katsura tree, *Cercidiphyllum japonicum*. The garden is architectural in the sense that, like a good building, its experience is three-dimensional. But unlike the building, the sensory appeal is copious, soft and, of course, built in.

He wanted his garden to be green, 'that most exotic of colours'. The question is, what sort of green? 'In a paint shop you don't just ask for green paint, you ask for one with a bit of blue, or yellow, or white, or black.' So, for example, *Rosa glauca*'s bluish leaves and purple stems harmonize with the grey foliage of a young *Eucalyptus niphophila*. Underneath the dull green and sandalwood brown of the rice paper plant grows a silver-white unnamed *Astelia*, sharp and spear-like where the *Tetrapanax* is all soft lines and gentle angles. The silver-green of *Pulmonaria saccharata* 'Argentea' plays off against the subdued blackish-green of hellebore foliage, which in turn one catches sight of in relation to the soft bright green of day-lilies and the leaves of *Brunnera macrophylla* 'Langtrees' and *B. m.* 'Variegata'. Here and there drift Japanese anemones such as *A. x hybrida* 'Louise Uhink' whose leaf form, although familiar, is so important.

While the two themes of the garden are large-scale foliage and green, there are nonetheless many flowers. There are metres and metres of choice hellebores that make the garden floriferous in late winter and early spring. There are roses (such as *R. glauca*), day-lilies, *Crocosmia* 'Lucifer' – a huge patch beyond the rice-paper plant – and many others. Although flowers can at certain times of year be your chief impression of the garden, they work by highlighting the summer-long variations on green.

The underlying soil here is clay. Richard is forever working on this by digging in manure that he buys at the local garden centre. When planting, he prepares

large planting pits with great care, again working in manure. Drainage is excellent because of the slope, and the plants that receive a lot of ground water because they are at the foot of the garden, like the *Bergenia ciliata*, adore it because they are the right plants for the place. Recently Richard has had an irrigation system installed, because many of the large-leaved plants come from damp habitats. In winter the only plants he protects are the rice-paper plant and the *Astelia* at its foot, which he wraps in horticultural fleece. The only serious casualty in recent years has been a tree-fern, *Dicksonia antarctica*, which was a great grief because its huge-scale fronds by the steps from the house were superb. A *Chamaerops humilis*, all sharp fan shapes, is a good replacement. Richard's planting shows how by selecting from the repertoire of exotic tropical specimens you can integrate large leaves into a sheltered town garden without having to install expensive greenhouse facilities.

Layers and canopies in a corner of Richard Partridge's garden.

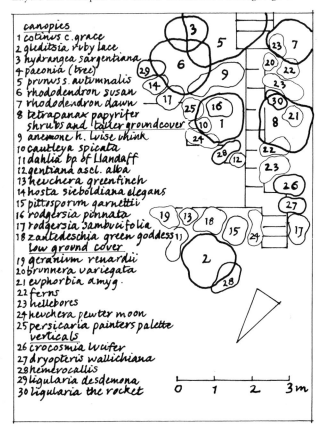

canopies
1 cotinus c. grace
2 gleditsia ruby lace
3 hydrangea sargentiana
4 paeonia (tree)
5 prunus s. autumnalis
6 rhododendron susan
7 rhododendron dawn
8 tetrapanax papyrifer
shrubs and taller groundcover
9 anemone h. luise uhink
10 cautleya spicata
11 dahlia bp of Llandaff
12 gentiana ascl. alba
13 heuchera greenfinch
14 hosta sieboldiana elegans
15 pittosporum garnettii
16 rodgersia pinnata
17 rodgersia sambucifolia
18 zantedeschia green goddess
low ground cover
19 geranium renardii
20 brunnera variegata
21 euphorbia amyg.
22 ferns
23 hellebores
24 heuchera pewter moon
25 persicaria painters palette
verticals
26 crocosmia lucifer
27 dryopteris wallichiana
28 hemerocallis
29 ligularia desdemona
30 ligularia the rocket

0   1   2   3m

Eric Ossart at Chaumont-sur-Loire

All the gardens in this section have related in some way or other to tropical jungle, but I would like to emerge from the large-leaf experience with another, sunnier version of the theme. After all, large-scale foliage has an important part to play in gardens with high light levels, as we noted with the huge, blue-green leaves of *Crambe maritima* in Derek Jarman's garden at Dungeness.

A festival of gardens began at Chaumont-sur-Loire in France in 1992. A framework of permanent shapes was laid out on a site by the château, where landscape architects and garden designers from across the world are invited to design gardens and to plant them. Some gardens remain for a number of years, others are changed more frequently. The site adjoins and is connected to the old farmyard of the château. Here the centrepiece is a *pediluce*, a beautiful old horse pond. To reach it from the festival site, you cross an elegant modern version of a drawbridge and walk between low farm buildings. In 1993 this 'corridor' was stunningly planted by the French designer, Eric Ossart.

The plants he used again and again, most appropriately in a farm precinct, were large-leaved vegetables. There was the swiss chard 'Feurio', a most beautiful plant with clear, dark red stems leading red veins into large, crinkly leaves. This was in stark contrast with cardoons, some of them wrapped in newspaper so that the stems would be blanched. Around these one bed was filled with yellow (tagetes and dahlias) and vermilion (another dahlia). The edges were packed with white busy lizzy and orange mimulus. Height came from cane tripods, for runner beans, and *Nicotiana sylvestris*, another large-leaved plant, obligingly successful in sun as well as in shade. Large-leaved cannas, green and dark, piled in the colour. This painting with plants was not precise and finicky, but free and loose.

The stars of this area, however, were the cabbages: frilly leaved ornamental cabbages, with centres either nearly white or lilac and white, the smooth grey-green leaves of what is really a red cabbage, tinged with a purple that went perfectly with nearby cobbles where the stone happened to be orange-tinted; and a crimped leaf savoy, darkish green and with a neat heart. This planting was simple, unaffected, colourful and beautifully judged for the somewhat bucolic setting and occasion. It was also emphatically French in that France has a wonderful history of vegetable growing. In 1885 William Robinson translated *The Vegetable Garden*, the fat manual by the firm of Vilmorin-Andrieux, and the result, with its vivid little black and white engravings as well as the descriptions, is mouth-watering.

OPPOSITE: Cottage garden or bucolic farmyard? Cabbages and chard organize the diverse energies of tagetes and cosmos. BELOW: Ornamental brassicas at Waterperry. At Chaumont such creatures were even more effective for being worked into composition with other leaves and flowers.

The Dry Landscape

PIERRE QUILLIER AT PARC ST BERNARD, HYÈRES, STEVE MARTINO AT THE DOUGLAS GARDEN, MESA, ARIZONA

Dry, like wild, is a relative term. The south of France is subject to drought only between May and October, whereas the total rainfall of the Sonoran desert in Arizona is only 18cm (7in) per year. Yet the dryness of both landscapes is capable of being seen either in a positive spirit, or with a kind of resentment, as though it were only a deficiency of water. The attitude has differed at different times. When John Evelyn wrote up his account of travelling through Provence in 1644 he says he found the 'rosemary, lavander, lentiscs and the like sweet shrubbs ... a very pleasant sight'. Passing through the country around Marseilles, he praised its vineyards and 'olive yards, Orange trees, Myrtils, Pomegranads and the like sweet Plantations'. He describes it as though it were an earthly paradise, a myth made real, with the golden apples of the Hesperides around every corner.

By the late nineteenth century things were different. Many wealthy garden owners saw their Côte d'Azur gardens as a place for their gardeners to follow horticultural fashion, cultivating lawns, growing exotics and bedding plants up until May, at which point their employers moved further north until the summer heats were over. This was a typical pattern of occupation, even in Russell Page's day.

Today the plants chosen for ornamental gardens can still imply a somewhat negative view of what the local pine-strewn landscape has to offer. Local councils have been known to spend thousands of francs on palm trees for traffic islands. The range of choice in exotics and hybrids is ever greater. Plants that are exotics in the north are natives here, and a vast number of species from the Canaries and Madeira will happily thrive most of the time. Opulence greets the eye in books on Mediterranean plants: bright bougainvilleas, vermilion canna lilies, campsis both orange and red, the intense clear blues of the tender salvias, endless bright yellow daisy-like flowers.

Yet taking a creative attitude to the local landscape and its drought-proof plants helps to resolve the question of choice, as well as making for gardening that is easier and uses fewer resources. The palette of vegetation native to the Var, east of Toulon, includes the reticent silver-greys and black-greens of olive and pine, the dusky muted tones of cistus and lavender. Hillsides light up with improbable yellow puffs of mimosa in February; all the year around lentisk, *Pistacia lentiscus* (the mastic tree), can make you feel that the slopes have been planted and pruned, for the shrub with the muted shine of its pinnate leaves and the flowers' pink shoots is neat and statuesque.

There is a growing awareness that gardens in the south of France that are created with indigenous plants can be extremely beautiful. But the garden I want to talk about is not in the private sector. Instead it is a public park, open every day, above the old town of Hyères, near Toulon.

Desert natives – acacia, saguaros and opuntias – are both stars and supporting cast of the Douglas's garden in Arizona.

Pierre Quillier at Parc St Bernard, Hyères

The site is steep, rocky and dramatic, with views reaching out to sea. At the top lies the famous house that Mallet-Stevens built for the Vicomte de Noailles in the 1920s, and the little 'cubist' garden devised by Guévrékian in 1927–8. Perhaps the notoriety of the cubist toy has blinded garden writers and compilers of guidebooks; for they never mention the terraces below, which Pierre Quillier has turned into an outstanding garden.

These five terraces date from the time when there was a monastery here, and old water cisterns from the monastic era lie underground. Flights of steps linking the levels bear out Russell Page's view that 'garden architecture can seldom be too simple'. A number of trees go back to the time the Vicomte de Noailles made his garden. One is a *Magnolia delavayi* in a sheltered corner at the foot of the site. Now it is a handsome tree you can almost lean over to touch from the parapet above. He also planted a group of umbrella pines below the house. These are now full size and anchor the whole place to the hillside, providing deep shade for high summer. They form a link with the native *Pinus halepensis*, which grows on hillsides in the Var.

Just as important are the olive trees on each terrace, not only for their wealth of associations, but also for their colour and the way their leaves catch the light. Their distinct and well-pruned shapes are unobscured by adjacent planting, although just occasionally one carries a climbing rose. Again they marry the garden to its native landscape, or rather what used to be the landscape along the hills, before so much succumbed to developments. They are a link with the deep past for the olive was introduced to the Mediterranean thousands of years ago.

Pierre Quillier has kept a few lentisks he found on site and pruned them. They provide an evergreen foil to lavenders, santolinas and lantanas. Plants native to

Bright and risky neighbouring colours work superbly in Parc St Bernard when integrated with the quiet silvery grey of olive trees.

the region are drought resistant, sculptural, often aromatic and equipped with protective leaf coverings that lead to attractive colours and textures. They are the back-bone of the planting, as if, like Russell Page, M. Quillier sees that the plants of the natural landscape along this coast in themselves form a garden.

Shape is a keynote of Parc St Bernard, given in the first place by the terraces. Looking up from halfway down you can see how plant form is played off against land form: at the top level a cypress, below it a loquat and down again a *Cotoneaster lacteus*. Shape comes, too, from the moisture-retentive plants of dry climates, like the spiky agaves and the aloes, that gravitate towards clefts in stone walls, where their rosettes provide year-round interest and the spikes of red flowers in early summer an astonishment. Into the gravelly surface, which is allowed in many places to run right up to the tall holding walls, M. Quiller has planted a

Big, bold mounds of sun-loving flowers balance the strong lines of cypress, terrace wall and olive tree trunks. Spiky leaves give energy to the composition, with many gentle cushioning shapes.

dasylirion. It looks like a green hedgehog with little twists of tissue paper stuck on to the spines, and is so striking that you are tempted to photograph it on its own before, back at home, staring at a print of a geometrical curiosity, you realize that its visual charm lay in its relation to the gravel floor and the nearby soft leaves of a melianthus. Echiums that start life as weedy-looking as a November wallflower develop to magnificent starry-patterned masses of 2m (more than 6ft) across, producing blue steeples of flowers before expiring. Lavenders, ballotas and santolinas grow into neat domes and cupolas. The native bulbs of urginea, that still grow wild on hills along the coast and flower

in late summer, throw up magnificently sturdy stems. These can be played off against a stone parapet, or a wooden bench.

Elaeagnus ebbingei scales 6m (20ft), so that leaning on the upper parapet, you have an additional plant window ledge helping frame the view out to sea. Elsewhere *Muehlenbeckia complexa*, whose small leaves and tangle of black stems can misleadingly suggest a miniature, covers a wall 3.7m (12ft) wall, turning it into a green sculptural block. On a lower parapet, half a dozen pots of bulbine, which has small spiky leaves and soft yellow or orange flowers late in the year, provide a rhythm across a wide view. The scale is such that if you decide to imitate the effect, you'll probably buy 25cm (10in) pots, but what you actually need is the 40cm (16in) size.

Long ago the stars of Guévrékian's cubist garden were pieces of sculpture – and marvellous they were, judging from photographs – but given this site and the climate, plants can provide the sculpture for you, communicating a sense of well-being that exceeds anything a sculpture park can provide. Because of the stony site there is a continual play between hard and soft. When clumps of *Iris unguicularis* (syn. *I. stylosa*) come to life in winter, the quiffs of their leaves contrast with the well-cut stone steps into the angle of which they are tucked. A winter-flowering buddleia, possibly *B. officinalis*, and one of Christopher Lloyd's favourites, pushes up in a corner between high terrace wall and descending steps, so that its sweet-scented, creamy mauve flowers are encountered at eye-level.

M. Quillier has an artist's eye for getting the most out of groupings of plants, such as the large-leaved acanthus casually growing at the foot of a fine-leaved asclepias. By February *Melianthus major* is coming into flower, with pink arching stems. On one side of it there is a low rosemary, and on the other the chalky white-grey foliage of *Teucrium fruticans*. The spikes of *Yucca gloriosa* 'Variegata' provide verticals and punctuation. Echiums are sometimes treated as the soloists they enjoy being, but they are also sometimes flanked by sheets of purple dimorphotheca (osteospermum). This draws out the colour implicit in the echium's foliage. A couple of square metres of the common snapdragon are corralled into a little stone-flanked bed where, surrounded by Mediterranean grey-greens and blues, they look as exotic as jewels.

Below the astonishingly steely blue-grey leaves of *Nicotiana glauca* growing out of a wall, which is what it likes to do in a Mediterranean climate, is a phlomis, its leaves furred and textured. Both these contrast with the trunk of an olive tree, at the foot of which grows the pale airy rose 'Princesse Marie'. In another place, a great spread of orange lantana sits between rough-leaved phlomis and a small pittosporum hedge, its leaves the ultimate in polish. Behind the lantana is an exercise in leaf pattern, *Solanum rantonnetii*, with the dark tints of that family, and behind that again is a large bush of *Acca sellowiana* (syn. *Feijoa sellowiana*), with soft evergreen, light-reflecting leaves. Reaching into this is a great mass of the pinky red *Pelargonium* 'Roi des Balcons Rose' ('Hederinum'), growing at the side of some steps; while across the step is the blackish foliage of a cypress. Such groupings make use of quite ordinary plants, among which the occasional rarity injects excitement. They work so well because they move around contrasts of hard and soft, dark and light, smooth and furry, horizontal and vertical.

Light in the region is exceptionally beautiful. Around the curve of the hillside, in Edith Wharton's old garden, planting that is careful but unimaginative and includes much bedding out seems to make little play with it. Pierre Quillier's plants by contrast, starting with pine and olive, constantly react with it and so are remarkable sensory experiences. There is a glimmer in the garden even on a grey day, while in May sunshine the planting enhances the veils of light that characterize this part of France. Pierre Quillier's awareness of light seems like a mental resource, and everywhere interacts with his choices.

Steve Martino at the Douglas Garden, Mesa, Arizona

If garden owners in the relatively well-watered south of France have been known to favour lushness in place of an indigenous sparer look, how much more has green been craved in the Arizona desert. A friend, posted there from England, watered her lawn daily out of sheer homesickness. She noticed odd looks from her neighbours, and when the water bill came in, she knew why.

Yet a capacity to pay the bill is, in the end, less important than the effect of so many lawns and water-intensive schemes on water resources. Moreover green gardens are not going to create habitats for desert birds and insects, because the plants that need the moisture have evolved in quite different food chains. In some contexts, green can stand for sterility.

What happens if, instead of regarding the desert negatively, you regard it as a rich resource? This is likely to be a major adjustment. The Sonoran desert has a hundred days a year when the temperature exceeds 38° C (100° F), and in summer the maximum temperature is well over 38° C (100° F). If you have been used to greenery, it is easy to regard the environment as a sort of wasteland. But at Mesa, Cliff and Marylin Douglas and their architect son, John, have, together with Steve Martino, created a garden full of plant, bird and insect life, that is also stunningly beautiful. Martino, one of America's leading landscape architects, works mostly in the public sector, and he has won many awards for his designs, which include the use of native – that is, desert – plants.

OPPOSITE: The creation of shade by acacias was a priority in this garden, as was the planting of trees (seventy-four of the them) across the site. At right are the terrifying stems of the ocotillo.

BELOW: Enough to make the designer of green landscapes despair, saguaro, opuntia, desert trees, *Encelia farinosa* and the bottle brush, with its yellow flowers, make a dramatic sculpture, enhanced by the low wall's curve.

The key to the garden at Mesa has been to use plants of the desert, which are enough to make the gardener from northern European or northern America despair. The basic tree and shrub population of northern Europe, although called 'broadleaf', tends to have small, fussy leaves. In the desert, on the other hand, the water-saving and protective coverings of the plants produce bold sculptural forms, dramatic in themselves and increasingly so when played off one against the other.

Giant saguaros, standing like statues by the entrance to the garden area, help to support bats, birds, reptiles and insects. The Douglases grow fifteen sorts of prickly pear, the pads displaying many variations in colour and texture. These round shapes play off against the spikes of the American agave, which look at home here in a way they cannot by the Mediterranean. There they say 'exotic', which is pleasant enough; here they belong. All these, and the aloes, seem specially designed to produce striking shadows cast on the dry stuccoed walls of the house, or on one another. Over such plants are brandished the stems of the ocotillos, the buggy whip, with their energetic lines.

Yet these plants on their own, however dramatic, would leave the scene meagre. They dovetail with the many trees the Douglases added to the desert vegetation they carefully preserved. Here the theme is that of acacia (*A. greggii* and *A. smallii* and *A. stenophylla*), palo verde and blue palo verde (*Cercidium microphyllum* and *C. gigantea*). There are shrubs either of the region or from comparably dry areas, such as the brittle bush, with bright yellow flowers, and the chuparosa, *Justicia californica*. Additional bright colour comes from *Bougainvillea* 'Barbara Karst' in the summer, penstemons and verbena (*V. gooddingii*).

The 'sense of place' provided by the plants collaborates with the architecture, which is full of Spanish echoes. The boundary walls are low and unobtrusive, more of a psychological marker than a physical barrier. The dry stucco is softly coloured. The heart of the garden is around the pool and patio, with its tiled floor. Plants, therefore, interact with the architectural spaces, as well as helping to mould them.

Planting, pool, walls and water: all have been thought out in relation to the light whose strength, together with the heat, makes the creation of shade a priority. The garden shows that it can be made – by native trees – without lavish irrigation systems. The desert light is as dramatic in its changes as the plant forms it defines. Fierce and flattening during the day, by evening it is rosy and deepens the various dusty grey-greens and browns.

The success of the Douglas's garden comes partly from concentrating desert plants in a small area. Changing desert light produces colour transformations each day.

Plants and Modernism

Arne Jacobsen in Copenhagen and Oxford,
Preben Jakobsen in the Cotswolds

Plants are friendly creatures. Modernism is a decidedly unfriendly and difficult term. So to pair plants and modernism may seem implausible, especially since the greenery that early modernist architects intended should surround their buildings in many instances did not materialize. However, Frank Lloyd Wright's Fallingwater is an excellent example of a modernist vision in which nature is as important as the building. The way in which trees around the house were preserved and weigh equally with the architecture is great planting.

Perhaps the main legacy of modernism to planting is that it frees us to see plants with new eyes. Plant form, which follows from the function of each part, is living testimony to the modernist tenet that form should follow function. A further aspect of modernism lies in its links with abstract art, and plants can be seen in the same way. Look at the teazle or the spirals of a sunflower head. And trees are living sculpture, be they old, windblown or pruned. One of the most famous examples might be the lyrical group of Californian live oaks that surround the abstract form of the swimming pool in Thomas Church's El Novillero near San Francisco. It is not necessary for humans to intervene. Stunted hawthorns may be sheared by prevailing winds into shapes rivalling anything created by Henry Moore. So plant and trees seem to be part of the world of abstract art, yet at the same time they still invite us to see, touch and feel.

Admittedly some early experiments in modernist garden-making do not have a happy relation with plants. Photographs of experimental gardens made in France in the 1920s and 1930s show a lot of concrete. The modernist iconoclasts who designed these gardens include Gabriel Guévrékian, creator of the famous

Trees preserved around a modernist building – Frank Lloyd Wright's Fallingwater – are just as deserving of the description 'great' planting as the creation of colourful borders.

cubist garden for the Vicomte de Noailles at Hyères (see page 121) where Pierre Quillier now gardens, in Parc St Bernard. The modernists were actually reacting against horticultural excesses of the late nineteenth century, and understandably so, for planting in the hands of the horticulturists seemed merely ornate.

William Robinson and Gertrude Jekyll in Britain had reacted against the same phenomenon, but they sought to cleanse the palate by going back to the inspiration of plants growing in the wild. Guévrékian and the other French experimenters turned to technology and contemporary design theory to purge the excesses of horticultural hybridization. Such early experiments are a part of history. In the longer run modernism has given plant designers the eye to draw out qualities of form and texture that may enhance the ornamental role

Californian live oaks (*Quercus virginiana*) around Thomas Church's El Novillero pool are the apotheosis of plant sculpture.

traditionally associated with planting. To be able to abstract from the clutter of a plant's identity, its prettiness and maybe its colour, and see its form and shape before plunging back into the sensory immediacy of planting is immensely liberating.

No wonder, then, that when you have a designer who combines a deep appreciation of plants with an eye trained to appreciate and work in the modernist tradition, you find great planting. And no wonder two of my examples stem from Scandinavia, where modernism always took a gentler, more humane form while assimilating Scandinavian traditions of craft.

Arne Jacobsen in Copenhagen and Oxford

Arne Jacobsen (1902–71) is famous both as an architect and a designer. His elegant, practical cutlery and light-fittings, for example, continue to be used years after he created the designs. He also made a fascinating garden for his house in Klampenborg, on the fringes of Copenhagen, overlooking the nearby Sound from which the place was separated by a windbreak of trees. Within the garden, planting was low, so as not to interfere with the view. Strong winds were a major factor; since they curbed the gardener's choice plants had to be capable of standing up to them and were therefore unlikely to be delicate and flowery. But the garden shows no deprivation because of this. Instead other qualities were developed, particularly shape and texture. Strong winds also made the creation of windbreaks within the garden essential. Jacobsen planted a series of parallel and overlapping hedges, using a larch, *Larix kaempferi* (syn. L. *leptolepis*). In the shelter of these delicate plants such as fritillaries flourished. In creating the hedges, he also formed a solid geometry, a foil for delicate irises, alliums and grass stems.

Being an architect, Jacobsen used plants architecturally, appreciating both their structural qualities and the way they helped to define spaces. He also adored plants and many of his textile designs were inspired by them. His craft was typically Danish, and an analogy for it lies in the textures that run throughout the garden. These express the skills of the hand that prune, shaped and cared for them as well as the gardener's eye for pattern. Their geometry works with the design on the ground, where a basic unit was provided by slabs of light grey Norwegian marble.

He was fascinated by the patterning that could be found in ground-cover plants, having a great fondness for small ferns, such as *Asplenium scolopendrium* 'Undulatum', *Adiantum pedatum* and *Blechnum tricomanes*, which he planted in sizeable groups. *Asarum europaeum* with its rounded, glossy leaves was another of his choices. Above such ground-hugging plants arched the leaves of *Polygonatum* (Solomon's seal). Large leaves of rodgersias were placed next to bamboo or other fine-textured leaves, while at a higher level he brought in *Hydrangea sargentiana*, with its great, soft green leaves. There were solid plants, such as *Viburnum davidii*, which grew into a great hemisphere, and massed bamboo. Insubstantial clouds of miscanthus and gypsophila added lightness. The biennial caper spurge, *Euphorbia lathyrus*, the most architectural of all small plants, was allowed to seed here and there. I am particularly glad he grew *Veratrum nigrum*, whose new foliage in spring looks like a Fortuny dress.

The species hydrangea, *H. sargentiana*, stars in this sheltered corner but would be far less effective without the surrounding events of leaf texture and shape.

St Catherine's College, Oxford: grass is grass, but it can also be effective as a geometrical plane, especially when it is adjacent to a reflecting water surface.

The function of the Klampenborg garden was to provide a private oasis. At St Catherine's College, Oxford, the planting complements and subtly softens a range of buildings whose primary purpose is to function as a college. They are entirely organized around geometry; even the specially made brick expresses proportions carried across the site. The lawn of the main quadrangle is a green disc between low parallel ranges of buildings, with two cedars slightly standing on it off-axis – 'because nature is nature' observes a guidebook. Actually Jacobsen intended that there should be only one cedar but when the specimen still looked seedy after several years, another was planted in the expectation that the first would not survive. In the event both flourished and are beginning to be cramped – a nice example of contingency defeating the designer! To the sides of this hedges run like walls parallel to the buildings. Their function is to screen functional routeways and bicycle sheds. At the same time the idea of using hedges in this way is slightly witty. Their tasks performed, they create little protected theatres of mixed plants. Planting at St Catherine's is ordered and spacious but not regimented. It assists at an exposition of spaces and surfaces, which can be watery as well as green, for a wide canal runs along the front façade of the buildings. This echoes the River Cherwell running in front of the college, while reminding us that while the river may be nature, the college precinct is something else. Planting elegantly helps bed the modern architecture into the river meadow landscape around.

Preben Jakobsen in the Cotswolds

Preben Jakobsen is a landscape architect who can with luck be persuaded sometimes to design a private garden. Coming from the stable of garden design – his father ran a successful business on the Danish island of Funen – he trained in horticulture, including a period at Kew. When he saw, in 1956, an exhibition of the work of Roberto Burle Marx, the Brazilian 'landscape gardener' (see page 94), Jakobsen decided to combine his pleasure in modernist design with landscape architecture.

Preben Jakobsen working with Richard Creed: the beauty of plant form and interest here harmonizes with the sculptural statement of pergola and fence of multi-dimensional slatted timber.

Richard Creed , a solicitor – and a skilled gardener – at Sherston, near Malmesbury, was introduced to Preben Jakobsen by an architect client. There then began the intriguing process of reconciling modernism with a traditional English approach to gardens. Richard Creed's house fronts the village high street. Here the minute strip of garden has been planted with a subtle colour theme of blue and lavender, enlivened by the pink oriental poppy 'Turkish Delight'. In the main garden at the back of the house, Jakobsen's vision sensitively collaborated with his client's wishes.

There is meticulous geometry and detailing here that is highly sympathetic to the dense planting in which plant form and texture are married to rich colour effects. The designer may have groaned inwardly at the sheer variety his client clearly wanted – nearly

500 species – but so knit them together that all one sees is coherence. Simple in its effect, and completely appropriate to the site, the design arises on paper from a sort of collage of overlapping rectangles that generate the shapes of grass, borders and paths. For these, concrete slabs by the Belgian firm of Blanc de Bierges were chosen. They go perfectly with the old walls. They have a slightly ridged surface, which means they are never slippery in wet weather, and they are laid so that the ridging runs sometimes one way, sometimes the other. The unobtrusive patterning with texture thus created is the perfect foil for the different sorts of textural interests offered by the plants.

Small trees play a vital part in the planting. Along the end boundary they can bank up to provide privacy or thin out to allow a view of village houses beyond. They are planted staggered down the sides of the gar-

Soft yellows of verbascum and achillea among light green and yellowy foliage bring out the warmth of the Cotswold wall. Ridged concrete slabs provide a cool colour contrast.

den, creating a subliminally perceived zigzag of visual energy. On the west side a *Robinia pseudoacacia* 'Frisia' shot up rapidly and within a few years was blown down in a gale. The blue-grey leaved snow gum beyond, *Eucalyptus niphophila* (a tree also used by large-leafist Richard Partridge) has taken life more slowly and, twelve years on, is handsome and still in scale. Another *R. pseudoacacia* 'Frisia' still flourishes on the east side of the garden, harmonizing with the neat fence of vertical timbers stained reddish-brown that encloses the garden's working area. Such detailing is a hallmark of Jakobsen's work.

A typically handsome yet simple grouping consists

of a *Betula jacquemontii* rising from a group of broadleaved evergreens including a Portuguese laurel. Then other birches, such as *B. ermanii*, are brought in along the end boundary so a theme and variations develops. Many of the actual trees and shrubs were chosen by Richard Creed. This admirable example of collaboration between designer and client shows up in their good condition twelve years on.

The borders are mixed, combining perennials and shrubs, and thus possess a better structure both winter and summer. Creed already knew a lot of plants, but Jakobsen introduced him to a whole new range. These typically had qualities valued by the designer who thinks in terms of spatial relationships, shape and texture: *Phlomis russeliana* and *P. samia*, for example, euphorbias, grasses, rodgersias and soft shield ferns. Jakobsen planted a group of three *Aralia elata* 'Variegata'. His client balked at this particular expression of a modernist's enthusiasm for the abstract qualities of plants and took two out.

There are some wonderfully bold, clear colours, like the magenta of a *Geranium psilostemon*, and a yellow *Genista pilosa* 'Lemon Spreader'. Jakobsen enjoyed using some of Graham Stuart Thomas's classic colour associations, such as *Kniphofia* 'Sunningdale Yellow' next to *Lavandula angustifolia* 'Hidcote', and

Achillea filipendulina 'Gold Plate' alongside *Aster* x *frikartii* – an illustration of the way that choices of plant designers working in different traditions can be passed on. All these flower colours add up to the right intensity to go into the rather pale framework provided by the local stone displayed in garden walls and village houses. The stained timbers in the garden, both of the small working area and the pergola that runs along the end boundary, provide an enriching colour note that is missing from the natural landscape round about.

From the client's point of view, the modernist provided him with the hard structures around which he could enjoy his love of plants. Creed also discovered he liked Jakobsen's plant choices (give or take the odd aralia). From the modernist's point of view, Jakobsen made the garden more gardenesque than he would have done had he been working on a public commission, softening what British gardeners would regard as a slightly austere vision. As a visitor to the garden, I enjoyed the richness of the planting and colour in the borders, but also the underlying forms. Grass is grass; but it can also be green geometry.

The layout of Richard Creed's garden, showing the underlying geometry of interlocking rectangles. The zigzag line indicates the visual tension between trees planted on either side of the site.

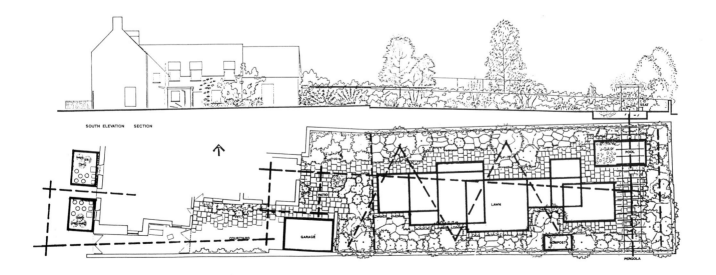

SOUTH ELEVATION SECTION

PART III
DESIGNING
WITH PLANTS

ABOVE: Against a floor of shingle and *Artemisa stelleriana*,
shapes of sedum and *Stipa* x *tenuissima* are all the more
effective. Stems of *Tulbaghia violacea* inject visual energy.

OPPOSITE: Shades of grey – artemisia and anaphalis –
are the bed-rock of the enchanting, painterly planting
in Ton ter Linden's garden.

Planting here soars to lift the spirits, as lavender, valerian and *Dictamnus albus* give way to poppies and *Crambe cordifolia*.

anning Roper was appreciative of all his clients. But he gently distinguished between those who were keen on plants ignoring design, and those who were interested also in contrasts of foliage, textures, shapes, colours and composition. Garden enthusiasts often start off in the former group. Plants are inspirational, accessible, relatively affordable and possess curious personalities, and there is joy in acquiring them. But somehow a passion for individual plants leads to planting schemes from which something is missing. They look so unlike those delightful vistas at Sissinghurst, and adding another pot, or another splash of colour, or even an extra flowerbed, does not work the desired magic. Often the plants, rare and precious though they may be, end up as individual items rather than parts of an overall design. This is a pity, because it is perfectly possible to have one's cake and eat it, to

enjoy plant character, whether rare or common, and to place plants so that there is an additional pleasure from the way they all work together and with other elements in the garden.

Plants are in themselves so well designed. You have only to take a magnifying glass to the smallest plant, said Russell Page, and 'at once, strength, will, design, colour and a tremendous rational simplicity invades eye and mind'. In addition, garden plants are spatial creatures, their leaves 'breathing organs in light and air'. Like human beings they live and move through space. To make the most of them in the garden, then, we need to approach them with a few principles in mind.

Structure

Structure and shape are fundamental to good planting, as to gardens in general. After all, in creating an agreeable living room, we start with the walls and the shape they define, and then put within them furniture shapes we find pleasing. In a garden some of the structure is likely to come from the 'hard landscaping' and garden features: walls, levels, trellises, pergolas and sometimes

The clearest statement of plant walls is made by pleached and trained trees, as at Dumbarton Oaks.

the house wall itself. Japanese gardens of gravel and beautifully placed rocks, such as the famous Ryoan-ji garden in Kyoto, show that a satisfying garden structure need not depend on planting at all. But in the West gardeners are more likely to want plants in the garden, and what they can contribute to structure is vital, for all that it is visual and physically supports only the plant itself.

In planting the main structural element is provided by trees. How these look depends on where they are placed on the ground plan. If they are to offer an optimally satisfying structure, a firm and pleasing lay-out is

The extremely structural planting at Mottisfont Abbey, Hampshire, has echoes of a monastic past as well as going perfectly with wall and urns.

needed so that there is a satisfying geometry on the ground. Hedges, a trellis covered by climbing plants and pleached lime or hornbeam can provide the garden with green walls. The hundreds of metres of yew hedges at Great Dixter (see page 109) show what a strong structure another type of green wall can contribute to a garden, delineating and guiding routes as well as providing a visual contrast with the adjacent, colourful borders.

Within any one area of planting there needs to be structure, even if we do not consciously think of it as such, for if there is no underlying structure the planting will look random and arbitrary. A wide range of plants of all sorts have architectural virtues. Deciduous shrubs and trees as well as evergreens contribute to the winter structure of a garden. The pleasing stems of a cercidiphyllum in December define space as effectively as a *Viburnum rhytidophyllum*, albeit in a lighter, airy way.

A further sense of structure is provided by the ephemeral summer growth of perennials. The structures of these, as of smaller shrubs, have a kind of intimacy, because we walk among them, that is different in character from anything that the larger trees or hedges can provide.

A case history in structure is Sissinghurst White Garden (see page 105). Box hedging in winter shows on what a firm basis all the sensuous foliage is built. The rose arbour, too, carries on the ordering of the garden's spaces, while the silver pear brings structure of a gentler kind to another corner of the garden. Needless to say, the garden has excellent 'walls', be they yew or brick or brick covered with a climbing rose.

Form, Shape and Line

'What is important to me in the garden is shape,' says Beth Chatto. The plants found in a ditch may present interesting detail and a pleasing overall tapestry, but brambles, nettles and herb Robert are, unless looked at individually and closely, amorphous. Shape in the garden is often to be found in built features or containers, for which plants are no substitute. Graham Stuart Thomas has two large urns in his back garden, but he does not plant them up, and rightly so, for plants would detract from their clarity. A large, well-shaped pot can bring to a planting area a form, a precision and a clear, hard edge that no plant can provide. The garden's visual effectiveness depends, as ever, on contrasts.

A shapely bench can enhance an area, as can steps and pergolas, and such forms can be played off against contrasting plant effects. When we turn to the realm of planting, shapes can be provided simply by hedges, but a more pronounced form is given by clipped yew, bay or topiary. Apart from such regularly groomed features, there are also the shrubs that, with perhaps some judicious pruning, make a good shape, such as *Viburnum rhytidophyllum*, or further down the scale the skimmias. Phlomis, for example, are to be valued for their slightly informal shapeliness, which makes their softly curved leaves and exotic flowers all the more effective. Rhododendrons, too, have a large part to play in providing shape: in a small garden, *R. yakushimanum* and smaller hybrids, such as *R.* 'Ptarmigan', can bring form to a stretch of planting.

A way to extend thinking about shape is to consider it as mass that may then be contrasted with a void. The voids are, in fact, as important as the masses, not only in functional ways as in hedged walkways, but in visual terms across the garden. To get the best out of

shape, we need to think it through in terms of the spaces between as well as the solid shapes themselves.

Line in planting, perhaps in the form of paths, can lead the eye through a garden. It can be provided by the outline of a plant mass, or by trunk or bough of trees.

In this garden by Oehme and van Sweden, the path's receding line contrasts with rounded, billowing plant shapes.

Pruning

This might seem to be a purely horticultural consideration, but pruning has everything to do with shape. Russell Page noticed one day that a *Magnolia soulangeana* he had planted twelve years previously was too solid:

> *So I began to prune it, starting rather gingerly, with a twig here and there. As I worked I realized that I was working with space, carving the empty air into volumes caught in the angles of branch crossing branch and held by leafy sprays.*

To prune is to be the sculptor. The pruning of even small shrubs and trees can radically enhance their visual grace – as well as opening up views afresh after midsummer and thereby animating a garden. Small trees have to be paid for in small gardens by skilful pruning, but the results can be extremely beautiful. Even a silver pear or a cercidiphyllum can ennoble a small garden and can look at home in a relatively small space if carefully pruned. The secret is not to shear back from the outside but to investigate what boughs can be reduced or eliminated within the total mass of the tree. Well-pruned climbing roses, too, have a poetic and sculptural dimension.

Of course, pruning is not a global prescription. It is highly inappropriate for desert plants; and as for tidying up the old and dying stems of palm tree leaves, the practice has been described as 'poodling palms'.

Pruning ensures that *Schinus molle*, the false pepper tree, makes a strong sculptural statement in this Californian garden.

Floors and Ceilings

We would not want our rooms to lack a floor or a ceiling, and we all give careful thought to floor coverings in the house, whether they are carpet, vinyl or timber. Similarly, the garden needs to be given a floor. It can be quite simple and does not have to be planted. Paving or shingle, which can be pleasing and functional, may be the most effective way of displaying adjacent planting. Perhaps your intention is to keep such areas clear for ease of maintenance, but one of the pleasures of plants is that they can enrich the floor. Camomile can be used to soften a York stone path. Plants enjoy seeding themselves into gravel, thereby imitating the way they grow in the wild. This is a case for 'creative weeding' as Ton ter Linden calls it.

A carpet of grass is delicious, and when a stretch of grass is taken over by crocuses in early spring the carpet becomes luxurious. Most such plant carpets are to be looked at rather than trod on: heathers, bedding-out plants, as well as the tapestry of plants that can be achieved in a woodland border. Christopher Lloyd and the wild meadow gardener are creating enriched versions of plant carpets to be found in the wild. The thyme by the moat at Sissinghurst is a fantasy carpet in which the colours are complemented by bees and their association with honey. In the Blue Garden at Parc André-Citroën a rectangle of bluish-mauve and silver is deliberately planted low to evoke a Persian carpet. The surrounding walls of the ramp walkways enhance it – just as comfortable furniture invites us to relax in our sitting rooms. In planting terms it is given point by the adjacent square of tall irises, lupins and delphiniums that have a vertical thrust and are the most intense shade of pure blue. Margery Fish's style of gardening at Lambrook Manor was to carpet the whole garden, ditches and all.

The delectable thing about a garden is that, unlike a room, it is open to the sky. The sky is the ceiling. But without plant canopies there is no shade and no

Canopies such as this are pleasing to the human spirit, while layers of canopies in woodland are ecologically fruitful.

contrast to make us appreciate the difference between open and covered. Canopies can be provided by pergolas, whether or not they are clad in climbing plants. More powerful are the canopies provided by large trees, which by reason of their age lie beyond our control. In the artificial circumstances of a town garden, they are likely sometimes to need pruning in which case the aim must be to lighten and layer the canopy. Even the pruning of a yew tree can be thought through in terms of turning solid green mass into a layered canopy.

Beneath the canopy of the large deciduous tree the

OPPOSITE: Meadow gardening is one of Christopher Lloyd's specialities. Rich in associations for the visitor, it gains even more by the contrasting close-mown path, with its sympathetic curve.
BELOW: Is grass just 'grass' or 'lawn'? Anthony Noel calls his a 'green jewel'.

gardener can choose smaller trees and shrubs that will enjoy the semi-shade. The well-canopied garden is exceptionally pleasing to the human spirit. Some smaller trees have a particularly delicate canopy, as users of Paley Park in New York know very well. Here the quality of the branches of the honey locust (*Gleditsia triacanthos*) lightly reaching out into space along with the presence of water create a magical environment.

The idea of canopies and layers can be carried down the scale, to the level of Solomon's seal stems arching over lower ground cover. There is always great pleasure to be found in the creation of a community of plants where each occupies a distinct layer of space, particularly in parts of the garden that at first sight would seen to be disadvantaged by shade.

Proportion and Scale

To make us feel at home, planting, like a garden's built features, must be in scale. We are not likely to have an optimal relation to a *Viola labradorica* or a giant redwood. Planting also needs to be in scale relative to the garden's size. We need to stand back from the planting we intend and visualize it in terms of the garden landscape. In general, we never make our gestures sufficiently generous. It is easy to be so absorbed in the qualities or the rarity of a plant that we overlook the question of how it will relate to what is around it. Getting scale right often involves being bolder, planting in threes or fives or sevens – or thousands! – to make a telling group.

But this is only one method and we could perhaps be using other planting principles. There is the idea employed at Westpark, Munich (see page 88), of a major 'parent plant' group and then notional 'offspring' spreading out. Another idea in large areas is to create a grid, and in each square to plant one particular species and build up a rhythm across the area by the way squares are filled in. The edges of the squares disappear as the plants become established, and the result is a satisfying intermingling effect.

The two ways of design in planting just mentioned derive from observing how plants grow in the wild. The scale of nature's planting is grand and planting in an open setting needs to take account of this fact, just as the scale of the landscape affects decisions within the garden. In Australia, gardens that respect the native landscape are likely to have wide, spacious, informal steps, that call for equally ample sweeps of planting to surround them. It may even be that the way in which the domestic European natural landscape dwarfs the garden is one reason why gardeners have often tended to block it out, leaving only a carefully controlled view. Wolfgang Oehme and James van Sweden (see page 91) encounter the scale of the American landscape boldly, planting great swathes of grasses. Thus the cultivated garden rests in balance with the larger landscape it leads into.

Scale in the small garden is particularly important. It is easy to think that because the space is small, everything must look small. Not so. The larger tree, shrub or climber can expand the space, as can large leaves. To keep everything small is to end up with fuss. Mysteriously, Myles Challis demonstrates how a small backyard can be nearly all large leaves, and still provide tranquillity.

LEFT: This generous but simple planting – santolina and wisteria – is in scale with Powis Castle's tall terrace walls.
OPPOSITE: Small gardens need not be limited to small plants. Hostas and rodgersias bring scale to Myles Challis's minute garden.

Rhythm and Repetition

'Rhythm is the most important single attribute in landscape design. It is the quality that gives life and joy, motion and repose. It is poetry and song.' So said the distinguished American landscape designer Will Curtis, who created the Garden in the Woods near Boston. Rhythm is what accompanies us everywhere in gardens, through our breathing, our pulses and our walking. The natural landscape is full of rhythms, as the photography of Bill Brandt and Fay Goodwin reveals. In the desert it appears in sand dunes and their ridged surfaces, while in temperate zones the rhythm comes from trees and hedge lines as well as from the contours of ridge and hill.

Gardens are places where the rhythm that is implicit in plants and landscape can be recreated, without inter-

OPPOSITE: Repeated stems of *Lavandula stoechas* take the eye through this section of Beth Chatto's gravel garden. They chime with the rhythmic stems of *Tulipa sprengeri*.
BELOW: The ingenuity of *Asplenium trichomanes* in finding a niche for itself in a wall seems to be expressed in the energetic rhythms of its fronds.

ference from concrete, tarmac and traffic. The point of most gardens is to reveal the passage of the seasons. The patterns inherent in the garden, as in music, involve more than one of our senses. The eye sees them, the foot treads them and stems, leaves and flowers invite us to touch and feel them. Planting, like music, allows our innate rhythmic sympathies to expand. While they may be expressed by the ground plan, rhythmical qualities grow with the plants. Think of the way buds alternate on a bough, or how a stem of *Corokia* x *virgata* zigzags its way between nodes, or how the veins of *Viburnum davidii* appear to spiral. Rhythm suggests energy and flow. It integrates the different parts of a plant into a unity and provides the eye with a pleasing and purposeful route.

Rhythm depends on repetition. It may, therefore, arise from a balanced planting of trees. It can be seen in the stems of groups of bulbs, grown in planters or in drifts out in the garden, or on a larger scale in the stems of groups of trees. It is a feature of the great arching branches of *Rosa moyesii* or a *Rubus tridel* 'Benenden'. It involves an alternation between tension and relaxation: the budding node concentrates energy, the length of the stem draws it out. It is the visible manifestation of a plant's physical energies and a major source of visual energy in the garden.

Certain plants display rhythmical vigour to a very high degree: Solomon's seal and smilacina in the shade, for example, *Schisandra rubriflora* among the climbers, and, in the sun, the branches of species roses. It is vividly expressed by the rounded, wavy edges of many hostas, where the repetition of leaves enhances the effect. Other foliage, such as that of arisaemas or *Helleborus torquatus*, rises from the ground in spiralling fantasies. Among more formless plants a hellebore or an arisaema can energize an area. By observing and even feeling such qualities in particular plants, the gardener comes to incorporate what the plants offer into larger effects. Planting in which rhythmical potential is realized is planting that will stir the spirit.

Texture and Pattern

Human beings use sight in two major ways. One is in focusing on more distant views, which, in a garden, might be formulated by a tree, a statue, an urn or some other device. There is a pleasure to be derived from looking out over a landscape and gaining a sense of distance. The other sort of looking involves refocusing on surfaces close to us, and it is driven by our appetite for textures. The only arts and crafts to come near planting in this respect are those of needlework, weaving and tapestry. Enjoying the various textures of foliage is rather like the luxury of embroidery's textural effects. No wonder there is a tradition of depicting gardens in needlework. But plants far outdo what even the most skilled needlework can achieve, both in scale and variety.

Some plants have large leaves that, seen close to, have an open, wide texture. At the other end of the scale plants can be extremely fine textured, whether we are looking at yew hedges or at ground cover plants such as *Euonymus* 'Minimus'. Seen from a distance, a hedge of large-leafed plants resolves itself into fine texture. One of the aims of good planting is to achieve textural contrasts. Traditional Japanese gardens are miracles of textural economy combined with richness, and they are a constant reminder of how far this quality of plants can be taken.

If ferns, mosses and azaleas such as are used in Japanese gardens offer rich textural resources, how infinitely extended are those of the plant palette to be found in temperate zones of the West. The variations available are almost limitless, whether we are looking for a fine soft texture, as in dicentras, or a coarse texture, as in *Viburnum davidii*. Barks and stems take this aspect of planting further, whether the bark in question is that of yew or of *Acer capillipes*.

Pattern involves organization and repetition, whether provided by brick paving, an arrangement of planters or by plants themselves. The eye lights on pattern avidly, so that plants of patterned foliage running through an area of planting are a great asset. *Euphorbia characias* is all pattern, as well as offering shapeliness in its valuable blue-green tones. In Beth Chatto's gravel garden (see page 81), the pattern element in a given area might come from bergenias (several square metres of them), euphorbias, phlomis and clusters of alliums, whose vertical stems create a different kind of pattern. But for all the plants to be patterned would be counterproductive, so these highly organized ones are mingled with looser, more informal species or thyme in which all one sees is fine texture.

Large leaves are often highly patterned, such as the palmate-leaved rodgersias or the simpler shapes of peltiphyllums and hostas. Again, the art in using them is to plant enough to make an impact in terms of scale, but to contrast them with fan-like leaf patterns or more informal-looking foliage.

OPPOSITE: The seedheads of *Allium christophii* are as texturally interesting as the flowers themselves.
BELOW: A shapely sorbus brings pattern and texture to planting, as well as providing autumn colour.

Colour and Light

Although many pages in this book have been devoted to it, it must be said that colour is not the most important property of a garden, unless we are to include green. Even then, gorgeous and subtle colours are nothing if not accompanied by a shapely structure. The colours we so value in garments would be virtually meaningless if there were not a human shape wearing them, and in the same way colour gardens that succeed have good, basic structures and planting that exploits the intrinsic structural qualities of plants. Successful colour gardens are those in which the colour is contrasted by quieter areas. Beth Chatto's gravel garden is a jewel box indeed in summer, but even here there are large areas of plain shingle and the large *Cupressocyparis leylandii* hedge to absorb it, not to speak of the many sorts of quiet grey-green to almost black foliage that are a major theme of the garden. They also work when colour relationships have been thoughtfully attended to. This is where the reader may expect the colour wheel to pop up, but handling colour is a matter of experience not of theory.

An excellent training in colour planting is to carry out some of Gertrude Jekyll's principles, noticing how an eye that is saturated with greys does indeed turn to yellows with avidity, and how yellows, in their turn, make the eye appreciate purples and mauves. Juggling with pots of plants can reveal how exciting is the effect of an orange-red placed next to a pinkish-red. Just what goes with what cannot, given variations in light and climate, be a matter of prescription. A fruitful principle is that each colour can be warm or cool, and that too many of one or the other will fall flat. A pale, cool yellow nasturtium, while lovely in itself, can also be put next to a warmer yellow, even embodied in a leaf, and the contrast will enhance each.

LEFT: Working within the same colour family can produce animation, as with these echinaceas and asters.

Different shades of yellow from tagetes, through to the warm orange of ripening tomatoes, mutually enhance each other in a matrix of green.

The colour that is most rewarding to study in terms of warm and cool is green. The play of warm greens – such as zantedeschia, epimediums, day-lilies, ferns – against cool, grey-blue greens – of *Euphorbia characias*, *Dicentra* 'Langtrees', *Hosta sieboldiana* – can take life and harmony across the garden. When the colour of paving is taken into account, the whole is enriched further. If my path were of warm brick, my planting choices would to some extent be different from those I would make were the material cool York stone.

The richest, most economical effects in colour are, I would suggest, when plant foliage is treated as a colour resource, and flower colour is used to provide highlights. It is remarkable how even in late summer a few flowers of *Salvia confertiflora* are enough to inject excitement into several square metres of various kinds of foliage. By experimenting with foliage colour, there need be no disappointing lapse in late summer, for grasses such as the pennisetums start to come into their own, and crocosmias, such as *Crocosmia* 'Solfaterre', bring in their curious grey-yellow tint, while artemisias look happier and happier as summer draws to a close.

A factor often overlooked is that different colours are appropriate for different seasons. Fresh greens, whites and creams are peculiarly spring-like. Warmer purples, yellow and oranges – the colours of *Clematis* 'Jackmanii' and the fruit of *Malus* 'John Downie' – are welcome in late summer.

Light, like shade, is a subtle component in planting. Some kinds of foliage reflect it, such as *Elaeagnus* x *ebbingei* and the ceanothuses, and others, yew, for example, absorb it. This fact can be used to develop contrasts, whether quiet or dramatic, between pools of shade and brilliantly lit areas. Making the most of light and shade depends on observing where the sun falls at various times of year and taking advantage of that knowledge. I once grew a clump of *Senecio przewalskii* under a yew tree where late the late summer sun somehow managed to pierce the branches. The seasonal planting was transformed, for the foliage is beautiful as well as the yellow flowers.

Solids and Screens

Some plants have an ethereal appearance, catching the wind and creating a veil of stems that half-conceals what lies behind. Such plants include many of the grasses – *Miscanthus sinensis*, for example – and the pennisetums, and, if you want a colony of stems, *Verbena bonariensis*. Others, such as *Viburnum davidii* among shrubs, and hostas, among perennials, are solid and relatively immobile in the wind. In some landscapes, such as those open American landscapes into which Oehme and van Sweden insert vast swathes of grasses, mobility is wholly appropriate. What is more pleasing than the sight of the wind ruffling a field of corn or a meadow?

In most gardens, however, the ideal is to contrast one characteristic with another. Beth Chatto invites us to half-glimpse what is further away through a veil of grass stems near to.

BELOW: Here the tall stand of *Calamagrostis* x *acutiflora* 'Stricta' acts as a solid screen, but airy grasses such as *Stipa gigantea* can also produce filmy vertical transparent screens.

Inside-Outside

Are we outside or inside in a garden? Outside, of course, but there are points in many gardens where there is a kind of ambiguity. It occurs most markedly as the garden meets the house, and there is a special pleasure to be found here.

The porch at Dumbarton Oaks is a beautiful example of the play that can be achieved between inside and outside.

The play needs to be begun by intelligent architecture, whether porch or atrium, or minimally by large, glass windows, or by an overhang that projects into the garden. Thereafter planting can enhance the effect. If there are steps, well-placed and sufficiently large pots and planters can appear to take the outside world of air and plants back into the house. There is also something of an inside-outside situation between a rose arbour or some other illusory garden room and the more open garden around.

Soft and Hard

The intrinsic softness of plants and foliage asks to be contrasted with hard materials, whether brick, stone or ceramic and whether garden feature or adjacent architecture. Plants and the garden path are a case in point. York stone is a matt, cool and sometimes cold grey; bergenia leaves are warm with a soft gleam and come in all shades of green with tints from coral to claret. The two show each other off admirably, the paving enhancing the texture and colour of the leaves, the leaves enhancing those same qualities of the path. In the same way, fine-textured box is an admirable foil for the coarser texture of brick.

Some of the most pleasing conjunctions of paths and plants are those in which the plants burgeon over the path's hard edge, hiding it for much of its length. The eye enjoys following an edge that is sometimes lost and sometimes found.

A major aspect of the contrast between hard and soft lies in the relation between plants and architecture. Received wisdom has long been that planting around the house should be more intense in interest while it should become less formal further away. Such a contrast ensures progression and gives planting a dynamic.

Planting by the house should, of course, match the building material. Beatrix Farrand, for example, gave careful thought to the plants that would enhance the brick of the garden front of Dumbarton Oaks and those that she should avoid (see page 34).

Some sort of signal from planting by the entrance is often appropriate. Great bushes of cistus curtsying either side of the garden door make it clear that we are arriving somewhere. While a cottage may call for hollyhocks to snuggle up against it and a comfortable town house will invite more dignified formal plants, modern buildings may call for quite a different relationship. The clear lines of St Catherine's College at Oxford are complemented by planting that comes, for example, in the form of free-standing berberis bushes whose own form is shown off by, but does not interfere with, the building's uncluttered elegance (see page 130). There is a subtle dialogue going on between nature and architecture.

OPPOSITE: Planting, including hostas, makes the most of contrasts between hard and soft along this path of setts.
BELOW: Inside-outside: great mounds of cistus and a self-sown bolster of *Erigeron karvinskianus* soften a formal porch and marry it to the garden.

Looking at Plants

The trouble with plants is that although we may be in love with them, we do not necessarily see them. 'Wonderful plants,' said an expert designer to me in my early days of gardening, 'but rotten associations.' I was crestfallen, since I did not want to make a collection of plants – a perfectly valid aim in itself – but to make a pleasing garden. The education of my eye had begun. I began to notice how plants need to be foils to one another and to work with their surroundings too; how an elegant sorbus replacing a beautiful but formless rambling rose made sense of the plants around; how an old pyracantha could be trained and pruned to reveal inky shade beyond a sunny flower bed; how the eye can be led through a garden, not only by a strong perspective, important though that is, but by tree answering to tree, and by one pattern of branches leading on to another.

Whether a garden is minute or immense, planting becomes engaging when, in various effects of similarity and contrast, all the separate elements start working together.

The intricacy of this planting at Hadspen Garden is organized by scale and contrasts, such as those between billowing fennel, crisp artemisia foliage and the fine-textured gravel path.

Further Reading

Brookes, John, *Room Outside*, 1969

Brookes, John, *The John Brookes Garden Design Book*, 1991

Brookes, John, *Planting the Country Way*, 1994

Challis, Myles, 'A Jungle in Leytonstone', in *The Garden, Journal of the Royal Horticultural Society*, 1985

Challis, Myles, *The Exotic Garden*, 1988 (republished as *Exotic Gardening in Cool Climates*, 1994)

Chatto, Beth, *The Gravel Garden* (forthcoming)

Colvin, Brenda, *Land and Landscape*, 1948

Farrand, Beatrix, *Plant Book for Dumbarton Oaks* (ed. D.K. McGuire), 1980

Farrer, Reginald, *The English Rock Garden* (2 vols), 1918

Fish, Margery, *Cottage Garden Flowers*, 1960

Hansen, Richard and Stahl, Friedrich, *Perennials and their Garden Habitat* (trans.), 1993

Haworth-Booth, Michael, *Effective Flowering Shrubs*, 1951

Healing, Peter, 'The Priory, Kemerton, Worcestershire', in *The Englishman's Garden* (ed. A. Lees-Milne and Rosemary Verey), 1982

Hobhouse, Penelope, *Colour in your Garden*, 1985

Jackson, Sheila, *Blooming Small*, 1994

Jakobsen, Preben, 'Shrubs and Ground-cover', in *Landscape Design with Plants* (ed. Brian Clouston), 1977

Jarman, Derek, *Derek Jarman's Garden*, 1995

Jekyll, Gertrude, *Wood and Garden*, 1899

Jekyll, Gertrude, *Colour in the Flower Garden*, 1908

Kellaway, Deborah, *The Making of a Country Garden*, 1988

Lawson, Andrew, 'The Art of Gardening', *Hortus*, summer 1990

Lloyd, Christopher, *The Well-Tempered Garden*, 1970

Lucas Phillips, C.E., *The Small Garden*, 1952

Oehme, Wolfgang and Van Sweden, James, *Bold Romantic Gardens*, 1991

Page, Russell, *The Education of a Gardener*, 1962

Robinson, Florence Bell, *Planting Design*, 1940

Robinson, Nick, *The Planting Design Handbook*, 1992

Robinson, William, *The Wild Garden*, 1983

Robinson, William (trans.), *The Vegetable Garden*, 1885

Roper, Lanning, *Successful Town Gardening*, 1957

Russell, Vivian, *Monet's Garden: Through the Seasons at Giverny*, 1995

Scott-James, Anne, *Sissinghurst: The Making of a Garden*, 1974

Snape, Diana, *Australian Native Gardens*, 1992

Thomas, Graham Stuart, *The Old Shrub Roses*, 1955

Thomas, Graham Stuart, *Perennial Garden Plants*, 1982 (revised edition)

Thomas, Graham Stuart, *The Art of Planting*, 1984

Tunnard, Christopher, *Gardens in the Modern Landscape*, 1938

Underwood, Mrs Desmond, *Grey & Silver Plants*, 1971

Acknowledgements

I would especially like to thank Jill Billington, Marian Grierson-Thompson, Sue Whittington and my husband, Malcolm Turner, for their friendly encouragement in the writing of this book. Steven Martino was generous with his time and faxes, stimulating several lines of thought. Emily Hedges has been most resourceful in tracking down pictures I asked for.

The students of the School of Garden Design at Middlesex University kindly allowed me to use their survey of Beth Chatto's gravel garden. I am most grateful to garden owners and designers in Britain, France, Germany, Australia and the United States for allowing me to describe their gardens and answering many questions.

The quotation on page 25 is from Isabelle Auricoste and Hubert Tonka (eds), *Parc-Ville Villette*, 1987 page 46. I am grateful to Julian Barnes for the translation.

The quotation on page 67 from *Chroma: A Book of Colour* by Derek Jarman, which was first published by Century, is reproduced by permission of the publisher and the author's estate.

The publishers would like to thank the following for supplying illustrations for this book:

Bridgeman Art Library/British Library, London 12, /Private Collection, copyright Sir Cedric Morris Estate 54, /By courtesy of the Board of Trustees of the V&A 13
John Brookes 71
Country Life Picture Library 30
Design Press 129
Ken Druse 120, 124, 125, 126
Garden Matters 127, 128
Garden Picture Library /Nick Meers 70, /Jerry Pavia 57, / Brigitte Thomas 59
Lucy Gent 42, 47, 75, 76, 81, 117
John Glover 16 bottom, 25, 43 top left, 65, 66, 67, 68, 112
Marion Grierson 31, 140
Jerry Harpur 8 (designer: Gunilla Pickard), 9 (designers: Oehme & van Sweden), 18, 21, 28, 43 top left, 44 (designer: Deborah Kellaway), 45 (designer: Deborah Kellaway), 46 (designer: Deborah Kellaway), 72, 73, 77 (designer: Rodger Elliott), 78 (designer: Rodger Elliott), 80 (designer: Beth Chatto), 91 top right (designers: Oehme & van Sweden), 92–93 (designers: Oehme & van Sweden), 109, 110–11, 136, 139 (designers: Oehme & van Sweden), 152 (designers: Oehme & van Sweden),153
Anne Hyde 14
Jakobsen Landscape Architects 131, 132, 133
Noel Kavanagh 115,116 (designer: Richard Partridge)
Noel Kingsbury 23, 88, 89, 90
Andrew Lawson 2, 17 (Connie Franks), 27, 56, 62, 63 (designer: Sheila Jackson), 95, 118, 147, 148, 150, 154, 155
Erica Lennard 55
W Anthony Lord 1, 20, 22, 74
JC Mayer & G Le Scanff 119 (designer: Eric Ossart), 151 (designer: Eric Ossart)
National Trust Picture Library 52, /Eric Crichton 32, 50, 106, / Andrew Lawson 48–49, 51, 105, /Marianne Majerus 138, /

Stephen Robson 107, /Ian Shaw 141
Clive Nichols 15, 24, 41 (Connie Franks), 96–97, 99, 113 (designer: Myles Challis), 114 top right (designer: Myles Challis), 135 (designer: Beth Chatto), 142, 143, 149
Hugh Palmer 16 top, 26, 35, 36, 37, 58, 130, 137, 145
Jerry Pavia 38, 40
B & P Perdereau 10, 11, 98, 102, 104, 134, 144, 156
Nori and Sandra Pope 100
Vivian Russell 121, 122
Steven Wooster 6, 82–3, 85, 86, 146.

The garden plans were taken from the following:

Australian Native Gardens by Diana Snape (Lothian Books, Port Melbourne, Australia, 1992) 79
Beautiful Backyards by Roddy Llewellyn (Ward Lock, London, 1985) 114
Blooming Small: A city dweller's garden by Sheila Jackson (Herbert Press, London, 1944) 61
Bold Romantic Gardens by Wolfgang Oehme, James van Sweden with Susan Rademacher Frey (Acropolis Books, Herndon, USA, 1991) 91 bottom left
Colour in the Flower Garden by Gertrude Jekyll (Country Life Ltd/George Newnes Ltd, London, 1908) 29
Roberto Burle Marx: The Unnatural Art of the Garden by William Howard Adams (The Musuem of Modern Art, New York, USA, 1991) 94
Sissinghurst Castle Garden (National Trust Booklet, 1987) 53
De Tuinen Van Ton ter Linden by Anne van Dalen (Uitgeverij Terra, 1988) 103
A Visit to Giverny by Gerald van der Kemp (the plan was originally drawn for an exhibition held at the Metropolitan Museum of Art entitled: 'Monet's Years at Giverny – Beyond Impressionism') 60.

INDEX

Page numbers in *italics* refer to illustrations